A Grateful Life

The life story of a husband, father, and taco loving dead head.

By

Tom Powell, Jr.

A Grateful Life

CONTENTS

A Grateful Life

This book is dedicated to my wife, Renee Anne Powell, who encouraged me to write it. Without her, my life would not only be vastly different, but ultimately incomplete.

She has not only been my partner in life since 1997, but she has also been, and continues to be, the best possible mother I could want to our three children.

She has been handed more than her share of the ups and downs a life can give someone, and she has come through it all with an unwavering outlook on life.

Renee, I love you with all my heart. Thank you for tolerating this grumpy Powell man for as long as you have.

If I sell enough copies of this book, I will take you to those kick ass huts over the Indian ocean in the Maldives.

Who loves ya, baby?

PREFACE

I once heard the question: "If someone wrote a book about your life, would anyone want to read it?" That question has stuck with me since the day I heard it. I don't recall when I heard it, nor do I recall where I heard it, but it has stuck with me nonetheless. In fact, that question was the original working title of this book. To me, it serves as a template for how to live your life. In other words, make your life interesting enough for people to want to read about it, and you'll surely have lived a full life. I have tried to live my life in such a manner.

Sometimes the interesting, unique, and odd things that happen in one's life are self-made, and sometimes they are thrust upon us by circumstances beyond our control. In my case, as with anyone else's, I have a strong mixture of the two. I believe some of my life experiences are a little more off the beaten path than most people's, as you will soon read. We all laugh, love, cry, fear, hate, rejoice, and mourn…but we each do all these things for different reasons. We each have our stories to tell.

As with anyone's life journey, I've had my share of ups and downs, but where my stories stray into the bizarre lies is in the horror I lived through for a brief, yet formidable period of my life. And yes, "horror" is the correct word to use in this circumstance. I don't wish upon my worst enemy some of the things that have happened to me. That being said, I am also seasoned enough to understand that each of those horrible things that happened to me served as another block in the foundation of my life, and therefore, they are forever a part of who I am. Without each of these incidents, I would not be who I am today.

So, with a massive shift in my life, I began to ask myself the very question that I began this preface with…if someone wrote a book about my life, would anyone want to read it? I didn't know if anyone would want to read my life stories, but I knew I had some interesting tales to tell, so I decided to test that question and see how many people would actually read a book about my life...and this is the end result.

Parts of this book will make you laugh, parts of this book will remind you of stories from your own family, and parts of this book will turn your stomach. I haven't held anything back because that would be telling you only part of the story. You're getting the whole story...every last detail, no matter how difficult it may be to read, or how painful it was to live through. So here is my story...exposed for all to see. You might want to grab a beer, glass of wine, blunt, or whatever you use to round the edges. This story almost requires it.

Thank you.
Tommy Lee Powell, Jr.

"A LOT OF LEGENDS, A LOT OF PEOPLE, HAVE COME BEFORE ME. BUT THIS IS MY TIME." – USAIN BOLT

CHAPTER ONE
The birth of a legend

I know what you're thinking..."Legend? Is he serious?"
See...when you're the one writing the book, you can title the chapters
whatever you like, so I did. I love being my own boss. I highly recommend it.

Saturday, May 13th, 1972 at 12:13 pm...that's the day, and time, I got my
ticket punched to the show called life. No VIP seating or backstage access for
me. Nope...it was general admission, lawn seating only for this youngster.
Looking back, I guess it was fitting that I was born at lunchtime. Did someone
say tacos? It was the day before Mother's Day, and almost forty-six years
before I would begin writing my life's tale. I weighed in at a respectable six
pounds and seven ounces. Just your everyday pile of Powell perfection. I
mean, honestly...have you ever seen a Powell baby? We're adorable. Simply
adorable. Perhaps because of my birthday, the number thirteen became my
lucky number. It is also the reason this book has thirteen chapters.

I was born at Gottlieb Hospital in Melrose Park, Illinois. At that time, Gottlieb
was the hospital you went to when every other option falls through. To give
you an example of what I mean, while my parents were in the hospital having
me, a man came in with a screw in his foot. The emergency room doctors
removed the screw, and the man was getting ready to leave...when he
stepped on the same damn screw! They had lost track of the screw they just
removed from his foot, and never found it before letting him go. Not exactly
dealing with the "A" squad, if you know what I mean. It was known as a last-
resort option for decades, but that also made it more affordable to young,
broke newlyweds. Since my parents fit that description perfectly, that was
the hospital my parents chose, so, Gottlieb was given with the honor of
hosting my birth. Two short paragraphs into this book and you may have
noticed that modesty isn't my thing. Buckle up...I don't get shyer as the story
progresses.

I was the first child of Ethel Marie Powell, a sixteen-year-old girl who was not
planning on having a baby at such a young age, and Tommy Lee Powell, a
man in his mid-twenties, who was not ready to settle down. Neither of them
wanted to be in the situation they were in. I was definitely not a planned
blessing. Hell...they didn't even really like each other, so they definitely didn't
want to be having a child together. Life comes at you fast. I only missed my

parents wedding by three months. I always joked with Dad that I could've been best man at all three of his weddings had he and Mom timed it just a little better. I was the result of a one-night stand followed up by nine months of anxiety, argument, and debate among two families that found themselves thrust together because of my parents' carelessness. At one point, two of my mother's brothers offered to drive her to New York to get an abortion to save her the embarrassment of becoming a teen mother. In those days, you went to another state to get an abortion so the people where you lived didn't know your business, and teen mothers were frequently shamed. My mother debated the option presented to her, but ultimately decided against it.

The two families would meet, and argue, about whether the two crazy kids should get married ahead of my impending arrival. My mother's family was insistent they get married, while my father's family was less sure. As I've heard in stories, during one such meeting, while my mother's side of the family was pushing marriage, my grandmother on my father's side stood up and said, "Slow down…we don't even know if Tommy wants to marry this one." "This one" …what a way to refer to your possible future daughter-in-law and mother of one of your grandchildren. It really is a shock why the two families never truly bonded. The Powells and The LaFiuras were like oil and water from day one.

Eventually, Tom and Ethel would decide to get married, and they had a small ceremony attended by family and a few friends just ahead of my arrival. Even though neither of my parents wanted to have a child at that stage in their lives, there they were…married and walking out of the hospital with a newborn son, nine months after meeting each other, and not quite sure what to do. They also did not know that the son they were welcoming into their newly forced together family would be the lightning rod that would forever alter their lives in ways they couldn't imagine.

At the time, my parents were living in a small apartment in Bellwood, Illinois. Because we lived there for only a short period of time during my infancy, I don't have many memories of the place in Bellwood. Bellwood, for those who don't know, is a small suburb of Chicago, situated almost due west of the downtown area, along the Eisenhower expressway, or "the 290" as it's known to those in the Chicagoland area. It is a very middle class, blue collar town, like many in the Chicagoland area. Many of the places we frequented in Bellwood when I was very young would be tied to with me forever, despite my short stay there.

10

Mickey's Hot Dog stand, an old school, Chicago style hot dog joint, would become the go-to place for the family to grab a bite to eat, and it still stands on Mannheim Road to this day. Mickey's is where I was taught the great Chicago tradition of eating a beef sandwich at the counter, while putting your legs back to avoid beef drippage down the front of your shirt. If you are from the Chicagoland area, you know there is a proper beef eating technique, and to deviate from it is to soil your shirt forever with beef juice stains. Mickey's was owned and operated by the several members of the same Italian family, one of which was Josephine Neapolitan. Josephine, or "Jo-Jo", was Dad's girlfriend before he met my mother, and still operated Mickey's on a day to day basis. How weird is that? My dad was bringing his new son, who he had with a teenage girl, to the hot dog stand where his ex-girlfriend works. JERRY! JERRY! JERRY! Keep the name Jo-Jo in the back of your head, as she plays a far more prominent role in my life later in this book.

Lezza's Italian Bakery, which has since moved its retail operation to Elmhurst, Illinois, was where we would treat ourselves to an Italian ice, or where we went to pick up cannolis for Christmas dessert. I still make the journey to Lezza's to get cannolis for Christmas to this very day, and now my own children have come to love the classic Italian ice Lezza's makes. And forty-five years later, I'm still addicted to their Italian cookies. Walking into Lezza's bakery is like walking into grandma's kitchen. It is clean, smells amazing, and is always filled with little bits of Italian baked heaven. Man…I can smell it as I'm writing this. I'll be right back, I must run to Lezza's. I can't finish this book without Italian cookies. OK…I'm back. Mmmm…. pure heaven.

Given the close proximity of my mother's family at the time of my birth, and the fact that Mom was a teen mother who needed a lot of help from a supportive family, I became deeply connected to my mother's family at an extremely early age. And believe me, the help they provided was desperately needed. In addition to not even being remotely able to support a family financially, my parents were facing a long medical battle with their newborn son. I was born with a double hernia, which required surgery immediately after I was born. Not exactly what a couple of broke new parents want to hear. In addition to that calamity, I was riddled with allergies. The list of things I was allergic to include milk, chocolate, trees, grass, cats, dogs, pollen, bee stings, and penicillin. While allergies are more commonplace these days, my parents and doctors didn't know was wrong with me for a few years. As far as anyone was concerned, I was just a sickly baby. I was the Fredo of my family at that point. It wasn't until someone recommended to my mother that she take me to see an allergist that they finally figured out what my issues were. He would recommend treatment for my allergies in combination with a drastically altered lifestyle and diet. For a lot of my youth I would have to eat my cereal with half and half instead of milk. My Easter baskets contained white chocolate instead of milk chocolate. And my time spent outdoors in the lawn was kept to a minimum. Do you have any idea how horrible Frosted Flakes taste with half and half instead of milk? I dry heave now just thinking about it. Nobody understands my love for milk now that I am an adult, but believe me, it was highly influenced by the fact that I couldn't have it as a child. My treatment consisted of a monthly series of shots delivered directly into my back. I can remember laying on the doctor's examining table, face down and shirtless, screaming as he made the injections. I would dread going to the allergist's office for those shots. It was an absolutely horrid experience for a toddler. Something must have worked, however, because I am now only allergic to penicillin. In fact, I've owned several cats and dogs, drink milk every day, and had a long career in landscaping, so I'd say doc was successful in getting me straightened out. In addition to all of that, I was born with my feet facing directly out to either side. This resulted in me needing to wear leg braces for many years in order to straighten my legs out. Try to picture Forest Gump and his leg braces. So, in a nutshell, I was a sickly newborn with a host of allergies and wind-swept feet who was recovering from surgery right out of the gate. Yeah, baby…startin' life out strong! LET'S GO!

The day to day assistance my mother received from her family came from a host of many aunts and uncles, as well as my maternal grandparents. Everyone was living in Bellwood, very close to one another, so it just became a part of everyone's daily routine. We were essentially one large family unit. Later, my mother's family would move to Addison, Illinois, where I would come to spend a good chunk of my childhood, as I will get into in greater detail later in this book. My Aunt Rita and Uncle Roger bought the house in Addison, and my grandparents moved in with her. Elderly parents living with their children is a very common occurrence in the Italian community, and my family was no exception. You take care of yours.

Family support always came from both sides of my family, but my father's family was primarily located in southern Indiana, so they became the family we would travel to see a few times a year. Since the day of my birth, I have made the journey South along highway 41 more times than I can even begin to count. It was a relatively easy trek to make given that it was only a four-hour drive from where we lived, but as a child, it seemed like it took a week to get there. The highlight of the journey southward was stopping at Don's

Drive-In in Kentland, Indiana. Don's was an old school car hop with a mostly gravel parking lot and the old fifties style menu boards with speakers. For you youngsters, the closest thing you can compare it to now would be a Sonic drive in. Stopping into Don's and grabbing an ice cream cone was as close as a child could get to heaven on earth in my eyes. My father was absolutely addicted to their breaded pork tenderloin sandwich. It's the kind of place where your burger comes wrapped in paper. Just a classic American car hop. I have since taken my family to Don's Drive-In on our trips south, and it's still as good as I remember it.

From Bellwood, we eventually moved to Northlake, Illinois, which is where my first lasting memories are rooted. I still remember the house address...125 Whitehall. Back then, I thought it was the bee's knees. We had a house with a yard that had great hiding places for playing war, we were very close to family, and there always seemed to be a lot to do. Addison Creek passed under Roy Avenue just a couple blocks from my house and some of the other kids from the neighborhood and I would make our way down the side of the banks of the creek and catch crawfish at the water's edge for hours. Can you imagine letting your six-year-old play next to a creek a few blocks from your house unsupervised now? My, how times have changed. We would play on the large stone sign at the church around the corner from my house until the street lights came on and ride our bikes all the way up to the White Hen Pantry on North Avenue. I had a blast back in those days. The pure innocence of childhood is something I miss very much. Youth truly is wasted on the young.

The house itself was a tiny little two-bedroom shack. It had the smallest living room and kitchen you've ever seen downstairs, with a bathroom and a junk filled three season room off the back of the house that nobody ever entered. In the middle of the house, as soon as you entered, there was a staircase leading to the second floor, where one bathroom and two bedrooms were located. One bedroom was my parents, and one was mine...until my brother came along, and I had to share it. The weirdest part about the house was the fact that it had a large, square opening in the bathroom floor upstairs, that looked directly into the bathtub of the bathroom downstairs. That square opening was covered with a grate-style covering that allowed you to see, and hear, everything in the bathroom below. Very odd. I hated that upstairs bathroom, but it proved to be an asset from time to time when you wanted to hear what Mom and Dad were arguing about on the floor below. And there was A LOT of arguing in those days. The entire house was dingy, dark, and musty. To be honest, it was a shit hole. Nothing ever worked properly, and it was always cold. And since neither of my parents were winning any awards with their housekeeping skills, it was constantly filthy. In all honesty, if the DCFS of today's age came into a house like the one I grew up in, the kids would be removed immediately. Perhaps the condition of the house was the reason why we never hosted regular company. It seemed like the only time we had visitors was during a pre-planned party or the occasional unannounced pop-in. We never hosted our neighbors or friends on a random Saturday afternoon. Ever.

We were dirt poor. And not like today's kids who think they are poor because their parents can't get them the new iPhone as soon as it comes out. I mean poor as sometimes we literally went to bed without dinner kind of poor. I mean poor as in a majority of my wardrobe were hand me downs because my parents simply couldn't afford clothes and still be able to pay the bills kind of poor. I've eaten my fair share of government cheese in my life. In fact, much of our pantry was stocked with government issued foods or generic foods. Do you remember when generic items were in white packaging with solid black letters? Well, our pantry always had white boxes with black lettering. I became envious of my cousin simply because he had brand name cereal in his house. How pathetic is that? We never had a new car. Ever. It was always an old, run down, piece of shit car that would sometimes start, and sometimes didn't. As I said, we were DIRT POOR.

Every Christmas my mother would use flocking paint to make it look like snow had settled in the corners of the living room window panes and my parents would do their best to rearrange the furniture in the tiny living room to fit a Christmas tree. I believe the Chipmunk's Christmas album was played more times in my house than it has ever been played on all radio stations combined. Seriously…when I hear a Chipmunks Christmas song come on, I am immediately taken back to being six years old. It's my version of a Vietnam flashback. As you came down the stairs, you could see into the living room, so charging down those stairs on Christmas morning would allow us to see what Santa had left us well before our feet touched the ground floor. In my house, the gifts Santa left for you weren't wrapped, they were just left under the tree, so we could see every toy he left immediately. When you are too poor to afford the extra wrapping paper, you get creative.

Mom always had music playing in the house when I was a kid. Elvis was my mother's sex symbol in her youth, so I grew up with a lot of "The King" being played in the house. Elvis and Kenny Rogers comprised the soundtrack of my early childhood years. Before I was eight years old, I already knew that I had

14

to know when to hold 'em and know when to fold 'em. I knew when to walk away, and when to run.

My adolescent years in Northlake were anything but normal. Because my mother needed help before and after school, mom would wake me up at four o'clock in the morning and we would make the journey from Bellwood, to my aunt's house in Addison, where my grandparents also lived. I was usually still half asleep in the back seat, and always still in my pajamas. We used my aunt's address to enroll me in Addison schools, partially because of the assistance my mother was getting from her family there, and partially because my mother believed they were better schools. I would then go back to sleep on my grandmother's bedroom floor, curled up in some blankets she would lay out for me with an extra pillow, until she woke me and my cousin up for school. I would attend school, come back to my grandmother's house, and have my afternoon snack while doing some homework, before being picked up by mother, around six in the evening, for the journey back home. It was an exhausting existence for me at my young age, so I can only imagine the toll it took on the adults involved in this situation. So, while I knew some of the kids from my block in Northlake, I didn't go to school with them, so I never really had any friends there once school began. Sure, I had kids I knew on the immediate block, but as you can assume, their friendships grew through the bonding of being classmates, so I increasingly became the outsider. And even though I went to school with the kids in Addison, I never really had any friends there either because I wasn't around in the evenings and on the weekends to do the typical stuff friends do that live in the same neighborhood. This made it more than a tad difficult to fit in at school, as you can imagine. I had no group. I had no clique. There was no other kid in my same situation. Like I said...it was not the typical childhood. Not fitting in at that age is very difficult. Combine this with my outdoor allergies, and I ended up staying inside quite a bit. TV became my friend most days. I spent my days hanging out with The A-Team, Starsky & Hutch, The Incredible Hulk, and Tattoo from Fantasy Island. The plane! The plane! And I can't forget The Love Boat, Three's Company, One Day At A Time, Diff'rent Strokes, Who's The Boss?, Alf, Magnum P.I., Growing Pains, The Facts Of Life, and them good ole Duke Boys from Hazzard. Those Dukes...always getting into one predicament after another.

I ended up attending Addison schools from kindergarten through my seventh-grade year. I failed that seventh-grade year. It was when I began to completely give up on school. I simply didn't care anymore about school. I attended class, but I never did a shred of homework and I didn't participate in

15

the tests. I just wouldn't do any of it. As a result, I would eventually repeat my seventh-grade year when I moved in with my father, which we will discuss in more depth in an upcoming chapter. With each passing year, I became more rebellious. More of a risk taker. More of a problem. I was attending school with my cousin, Joey, who was a year older than me, and all his friends. So, in a way they were de facto friends of mine as well. But they were really his friends. I can still see most of the faces from Sable Avenue now, playing in the cul-de-sac after school. For my cousin, it was great. He had a nice neighborhood, full of kids his age. I, meanwhile, was bounced back and forth between the two houses so I never really had my feet on the ground in any one place. By the time I reached junior high, I was in full rebellion mode and I was out of control...for more reasons than just the situation I was in between the two houses, as you will soon read.

The weekends my father wasn't working were spent at the race track, when I was a toddler. Dad was drag racing and we were always at one of the local drag strips. U.S. 30, Oswego...you name it. In fact, I took my first steps at U.S 30 drag strip. The smell of the fuel and the roar of the engines became the white noise of my childhood. Dad planned on me one day becoming a drag racer like him, but that's not exactly how things panned out. While I was constantly following my father around in awe at that age, I never became attached to the automotive world like he was. I didn't really want to be involved in racing because racing was the thing that was stealing what little time I had with my father. To this day, I'm not a car guy. To be honest, I have never even changed the oil in my car, and I have no desire to. I know that disappointed my father to his last breath, but that's just how I am. I couldn't care less about cars. It makes no difference to me. Don't get me wrong, I am still proud of my father for his success as a racer. He did something he loved and was good at it. I tip my hat to him for that. Not many people get to do something they love as much as my father loved to race. Now, let's take a closer look at my family tree

Tom Powell Jr.

"ITALIANS ARE FANTASTIC PEOPLE...REALLY.
THEY CAN WORK YOU OVER IN AN ALLEY
WHILE SINGING AN OPERA"– DON RICKLES

CHAPTER TWO
La milla famiglia della madri (My mother's family)

My mother came from a Sicilian family from the west side of Chicago that would eventually continue to move further and further west into the Chicago suburbs. It was a large family that always did everything together, and every event seemed to be centered around a large meal. Go figure...Italians like to eat. They were close knit, loud, and knew how to have a good time. The holidays were always, shall we say, off the chain. You couldn't walk five feet in any direction without coming across more food. It was everywhere, and it was glorious. Imagine every party scene in the movie "The Godfather," only on a much smaller scale. That was pretty much how every family party or holiday was like during my childhood when we were with my mother's side of the family. Italians as far as the eye could see, and every last one of them drinking, eating, and having a grand old time. Even the traditional American holiday meals always started out with a first course of Manicotti and ended with Italian cookies and cannolis. When the family events were in full swing, my grandfather would break out the "Dago Red" wine for all to share. He kept it in a glass jug with the rest of the liquor in an octagon shaped end table that opened to expose a storage cavity within. No matter what the event was, the smell of homemade Italian cooking hung in the air. It permeated every nook and cranny of the house for days after the party ended. What a wonderful time. That is the kind of smell that never leaves you.

The patriarch of the family, my grandfather, was born in Palermo, Sicily, and immigrated to America around the age of nine. He was born Gaetano (pronounced guy-ta-no) LaFiura, but when he passed through Ellis Island, he was given the name Thomas LaFiura, and would, from that day on, be known as Thomas Gaetano LaFiura. He was a short, proud man with very distinctly Italian features. His face showed the years in every wrinkle and scar, but he still had a smile that could melt the hardest heart. I don't recall many summer days when he wasn't relaxing in the back yard with a hanky in his hand to wipe the sweat from his forehead. Through the nearly see through fabric of his button down short sleeved shirts, one could clearly see the pack of Camel filterless cigarettes he always carried. Those Camels gave him an unmistakable bark of a cough that could be heard throughout the house. When the occasion presented itself to go out on the town, his fedora was the ultimate accessory. His hair was balding, and he had a tightly trimmed, grey mustache. As children, he would take our hands and run them across his face, against the grain of his unshaved whiskers, so we could get that feel of stubble that tickled our hand. He came from a time when you didn't wear jeans and a T-shirt. Even his casual "around the house" clothes were slacks and a button-down shirt. To him, jeans are what men wore while at work for a construction company, not what people wear around on a day to day basis.

He supported his family by driving a cab in Chicago. While he was a man that could've been so much more than a cab driver, he was content with a hard day's work to put a roof over his family's head. He was a great man. A true family man. Due to the connections he made working in the city, we would get visits once a month from "Manny the Greek." Manny was a guy that sold just about everything you could imagine on the black market. He would drive his station wagon out from the city and make the rounds. It would be filled to the brim with all manner of items that just so happened to fall off a truck at some point in time. In those days, a lot of things fell off trucks, and people were always looking for a deal. Do you need a toaster? Manny has one. In need of a new dress? There are a few in Manny's car for sale. Shoes, pants, jewelry…you name it, Manny had it. When Manny would arrive, the whole family would race out to his car to see what kind of goods he had this time, and Grandpa would be right behind us with a pocket full of money. That's how we shopped back in the day. Grandpa knew all the right guys, so anytime you mentioned that you needed something, grandpa would tell you he "had a guy." It's good to have a guy. Everyone needs a guy.

To say he spoiled his children and grandchildren would be an understatement. He would make sure each of his daughters had a big box of chocolates every Valentine's Day, and he would give his sons and grandsons sips of wine when Grandma wasn't looking. After he had a couple of glasses of Vino for himself, he would occasional break out a Playboy and let the grandsons have a peek. Eventually, my cousin and I would muster enough courage to sneak a peek without him, much to Grandma's dismay. He is the one from whom I learned the fine Italian tradition of grabbing a piece of bread and dipping it into the sauce as you walked past the pot...something I still do to this day. I mean, how can you possibly walk past a pot of sauce bubbling away and NOT dip a piece of bread into it? It's unthinkable.

My grandfather would often take naps in a lawn chair under his favorite tree in the backyard while enjoying a nice summer breeze in the shade. He was definitely a man that enjoyed the simple pleasures in life. I can still see his hand, where he was missing his pinky finger, and the tattoo of the Indian woman on the inside of his forearm. That tattoo also came with a story. As my grandfather tells it, one day he was jumped by two men in suits in the city. They roughed him up pretty bad. They thought he was someone that owed a local wise guy some money, and because he looked like the man they were searching for, he got targeted. But in the process of getting tuned up, his shirt ripped open, and the men saw his tattoo and realized they had the wrong man. They brought him to a local hospital and dropped him off. The next day, the two men visited him in the hospital and asked if he knew who they were. He said yes and explained that they were the men who put him in his current situation. They then placed a thousand dollars on the hospital bed and said, "You never saw us." He thought it was odd, but, hey, a grand is a grand. The next day, they visited him again, only this time, they placed a thousand dollars on the bed first, and then asked him if he knew who they were. He said no, and they left, and again he pocketed the grand. They paid him one last visit the following day, and once again they placed a thousand dollars on the bed and asked him if he knew who they were. He told them no

21

and said he was wondering why strangers would keep bothering him. They left, never to be heard from again. Now…that's how my grandfather tells it, so it may or may not be true...but it's still a hell of a story.

Eventually, his health would fail him, and in the end, his mind failed him as well. During his last days he barely recognized anyone. It was almost unbearable to watch my grandfather not recognize my grandmother, and then to see the pain on her face knowing what was happening to him. Knowing the end was so very close at hand. I still remember his hospital room, and him not being able to recognize my mother as she stood there weeping. To this day I still don't understand why, but I was one of the few people he recognized right to the end. I remember my mother telling me I had to get to the hospital because he was specifically asking where I was. I miss that man dearly. I could really use one more chat in the summer shade with him. And I know he would be spoiling my children rotten if he were here today.

My grandmother on my mother's side was Mary Lou LaFiura and was originally from a small Indiana town called Clinton. She had been married before my grandfather, from which she had two children, Minah and Donnie. When she married my grandfather, she had six more children, Thomas (Butchy), Leonard (Leo), Joseph (Joe Guy), Michael, Ethel (my mother), and Rita. Needless to say, she did her part to help carry on the human race. The woman was basically a baby making machine. She was a short, stockier woman who would work around the house all day in her nightgown. The disheveled early morning look on her face would last until her second cup of coffee, and all the grandkids were out of the house for the day. Grandma never drove a car. She was from that old school mold of women who stayed home and took care of the house, and therefore never had a need to drive. I couldn't possibly imagine not being able to drive, but she was happy not being out on the road. In her mind, her place was at home, and she did an amazing job of keeping that house running.

She was everything to me in those early years. She was the last face I saw before leaving for school and was the one getting me off the bus. She would stand in the doorway and watch us get on the bus, and the bus driver would always have a smile and a wave for her as she rounded the long island down the center of the cul-de- sac. Grandma always went above and beyond for her family, especially us grandkids. And man, she could cook her ass off. She may not have been born Italian, but she sure took to the Italian way of cooking after marriage, and let me tell you, she nailed it. Grandma always kept the cabinet under the sink stocked with a million boxes of cereal and was always ready to make us cinnamon sugar toast. She enjoyed the few times when she had a chance to get dressed up and step out on the town for a night. And she cleaned up nicely, too. Tom and Mary Lou made for a snappy couple at any given event back in the day.

Grandma had an old rocking chair next to her bed, near a window, where she would watch her soap operas while awaiting the grandkids arrival on the afternoon school bus. And when she was in the midst of a marathon cooking session in the kitchen, she would be watching her soaps, or The Donahue Show, on a small, countertop black and white TV. Everyone up and down Sable Avenue knew Mary Lou. She had an infectious personality. I think one of the things that made her so likable was the way she made everyone feel like she was their own grandmother. When I look back at it today, in a way, she was the grandmother to every kid in that neighborhood.

As kids tend to do, they have specific, and sometimes odd, names for the important people in their life, and I was no exception. She was always referred to as "Grandma The Big One." Don't ask me why, because I still don't know to his day why I called her that, but that's what she was called. It especially baffles me considering how small she actually was. Basically, my maternal grandparents were just large dwarfs. Small in stature, but could own any room they were in.

My Aunt Rita was the next most influential person in my life from my mother's side of the family. My aunt is who my grandparents lived with, and was the sibling my mother was closest to, so I got a heavy dose of Aunt Rita in my childhood. Aunt Rita married Roger Kazmierczak, from the land of cheese...Wisconsin. They had two children, Joey (who is the cousin referenced earlier), and Mary, who was born fourteen years after Joey was. So, while Joey and I grew up almost as brothers, Mary grew up almost as an only child, given the large age gap between her and her brother. Aunt Rita is my godmother, and she always made sure she was there for me. I didn't know it then, but she was a very hard-working woman. She started out as a secretary for a food importing company right out of high school, and eventually worked her way up to be vice-president of the company. She is a very accomplished woman. My Uncle Roger worked in accounting for a manufacturer of spray nozzles and absolutely lived for his beloved Green Bay Packers. It was an interesting marriage considering my aunt was a die-hard Bears fan. Let's just say that rivalry week was an intense time in their house. But their love was undeniable, and it shows in the fact that they are still together after all these years. All the ups and downs. All the family turmoil. None of it ever shook their marriage. That's a testament to them both.

Aunt Rita and Uncle Roger were the hip aunt and uncle. They were always up on the latest fads and fashions and always seemed to be in style. They were very smart about their spending, and as a result, had far more material things than we did. While we were dirt poor, they were doing OK. They took regular vacations and drove nicer cars. Their house was always clean, and nothing was ever in disrepair. I was so jealous of the life they had when I was a child. They had everything I wanted. Why did they have everything while I had nothing? The difference between the two families was noticeable. I hated being the poor cousin. I was mad that I was the one who always marveled at what they had while going back to my lower-class life.

Aunt Rita and Uncle Roger were also the ones that hosted every party and holiday. Damn near every one of my very early Thanksgiving, Christmas, Easter and Mother's Day days were spent at their house. Aunt Rita's house is where tradition became an integral part of who I am. She always did Thanksgiving and Christmas dinners the same way every year, so it became a very stabilizing factor in my life. When I was sitting at that dining room table with that specific meal in front of me, I knew I was "home." That safe feeling of family is a big reason why I am so tradition-driven now. Along my mother's branch of the overall family tree, my Aunt Rita was, by far, the most stable one of the bunch.

My four uncles on my mom's side have all since passed. I never knew Leo and Michael, as one died before I was born, and the other died when I was very young. I've seen many pictures of both of them, and as you would imagine, the Sicilian genes ran strong in them. Leo served in the Navy and Michael would be my mother's inspiration in naming my little brother. In fact, she claimed her dead
brother Michael appeared to her while she was pregnant, hovering over her while she was in bed. Years later, when my Aunt Rita would give birth to my cousin, Mary, she would needle my mom by saying the inspiration for Mary's name came to her when the Virgin Mary appeared over her one day while she was in bed. That joke drove my mother nuts. You have to admit, it's a pretty good joke. After all, Mom was always so dramatic about it.

My Uncle Butchy was said to have died in Arizona. As the story goes, he died in his apartment and wasn't found for several days. He was supposedly decomposed so badly, he had to be shipped home in an air tight tube and

24

have a closed casket ceremony. I remember this devastating my grandmother. She had lost yet another son, and this time she wasn't even able to view the body. She had no closure. It tore her apart. I sound doubtful of the official story because years later, when I was in my twenties, I met a man that claimed to know my uncle, and said he was still alive and well. When I brought this information to my family's attention, Aunt Rita seemed intrigued, but nobody ever investigated it further, and it was never spoken about. At the end of the day, Uncle Butchy was, shall we say, shady at best, so the story is extremely plausible.

One distinctive memory I have of my Uncle Butchy happened at my Aunt Rita's house when I was a very small boy and my brother was just a toddler. We had stopped over to my Aunt Rita's house for some unknown reason, only this time things were a little tenser. Dad and Uncle Butchy were arguing about something and things were getting heated. Before I knew it, my father told me to take my brother to the car. We had a station wagon at the time and my brother and I would climb all the way in the back and play with our toys. While we were back there playing, my father came out of the house, soon followed by Uncle Butchy. Butchy claimed Dad owed him money, and Dad claimed he re-paid the money already and was accusing Butchy of being too drunk to remember. As Dad
climbed into the driver's side door to get us the hell out of that scene, Butchy climbed into the passenger side door and began pummeling my father. Dad was no match for Butchy, so unless someone was going to help my father, he was going to take the ass whoopin' of a lifetime that day. Within seconds, Butchy was being pulled out of the car by a combination of my mother's family members, including my then pregnant Aunt Rita. Aunt Rita would later miscarry that pregnancy, and I still don't know if this incident was a factor in that outcome. Dad regained his composure, started the car and floored it. We sped away from my aunt's house as fast as he could possibly drive. What I would later learn is that before my father exited the house, he had called the police. They arrived just after we had left the neighborhood, and my Uncle Butchy squared off with them in the front yard. He had retrieved a shotgun from the house and was preparing to face off with the cops, before returning his sights on hunting my father down. The result of the confrontation between Butchy and the police was Butchy being shot multiple times and needing to be hospitalized. This side of the family was anything but drama-free and when the LaFiura boys screwed up, they made sure they took it all the way. Oddly enough, many, many years later I would find myself helping my father and stepmother replace the flooring in the covered back porch of their home in Berwyn. As we removed the floor, we discovered that newspapers had

been used as insulation, as was common practice back then. The first newspaper we uncovered just so happened to be the newspaper that covered my uncle's shooting, and it was open to that exact story. Talk about a small world.

My Uncle Joe Guy was awesome. A true man's man. He had his share of party days in his youth, but eventually went on to become a roofer, a husband, and a father to my cousin, who is the one member of the family who carries on my grandfather's name, Thomas LaFiura. Uncle Joe Guy was the uncle who took you fishing and talked to you about girls. In other words, he was the cool uncle. He was tall, tan, and as handsome as the day is long. Everywhere he went, he got second glances. His smile could charm the pants off a nun. I can honestly say that in most of my memories of him, he was smiling. He really knew how to enjoy life. I remember his green bass boat that was parked in our driveway in Bellwood. I would climb into that boat and pretend I was racing across the water for hours on end. At parties, his laugh could be heard from every room. Wherever Uncle Joe Guy was, he was holding court and he had people hanging on his every move. He eventually had a heart attack at a young age, leaving behind his widow and small son. He would be the fourth son my grandmother would ultimately bury. Nobody should have to bury one of their children, let alone four of them. I have missed that man dearly over the years.

One story I remember involving my Uncle Joe Guy was when he assisted my parents in picking up a used washing machine. The three of them headed out one night in my uncle's pick-up truck to get the washer. I begged for me and my little brother to go because I wanted to ride in the back of the pick-up truck, which was common then. They refused and told me to stay home and watch my brother. I was very little at the time, but they figured they were just going to be gone for a few minutes, so it would be OK. A knock came on the door a few hours later. I answered it to find two Northlake cops on our front porch. They were there to sit with us until family arrived. On their way home, my uncle and parents got t-boned by a larger truck. They found the washing machine almost three blocks away. Dad was shaken and bruised, and Mom had a pop knot on her forehead big enough for a calf to suck on. I've never been so glad to be denied a ride in the bed of the truck. Had we gone along for the ride, my brother and I surely would've been killed in the accident.

The two cousins on my mom's side that were out of state who we visited the most were Mineka and Joy. They were family from my grandmother's first marriage. Visiting Uncle Ken, Aunt Minah, Mineka, and Joy was always an exciting time. The trip to their house in Ohio was long, but worth it. They had a large piece of land, and Uncle Ken would always take turns driving us around the yard on his riding lawn mower. Uncle Ken was also the man who taught me the fine art of snipe hunting. I remember sitting in the woods that ran alongside their property for hours with a burlap sack, in the dead of night, listening to the sounds of the adults banging pots and laughing their asses off. In retrospect, their belly aching laughter should've been a red flag to us that we were being had. Aunt Minah very much reminded me of my grandma. She looked like her, was built like her, and had her smile. She was always so welcoming to all of us each visit we made and was always sad to see us go. My cousin Joey and I would play with Mineka and Joy for hours on end. Mineka has since gone on to have a few kids of her own, and she has defied Ohio logic by putting down roots along the western banks of Lake Michigan in Ohio's biggest rival state, Michigan. I love my cousin dearly, but her social media posts about Ohio State football sometimes give me the urge to drive to Michigan to whack her upside the head. Joy has relocated to Cincinnati where she has a family and successful business of her own. Social media has made it possible for me to keep in touch with them in ways we never imaged before, and for that, I'm thankful. Mineka and Joy, I'd love to arrange a weekend where we all took our families to King's Island one more time together.

Of course, there were many others in my mother's very large Sicilian family. Almost too many to mention. There was Uncle Joey, Aunt Marge, Patty Boy, and, of course, Aunt Gertie. Uncle Joe Guy's son, Thomas, lives in Colorado, and from what I can tell via social media, he is living a proper hippie life, making sure to experience everything this world has to offer.

Long gone are the days of the huge family gathering, with Sicilians in every corner of the house, and Entenmann's coffee cake for everyone to enjoy (That one was for you, Sebastian Maniscalco), but the memories of those times live on forever.

"THE ONLY PLACE IN THE WORLD WHERE NOTHING HAS TO BE EXPLAINED TO ME IS THE SOUTH." – WOODROW WILSON

CHAPTER THREE
My daddy's kin

Like my mother's family, my father's family was large, with many aunts, uncles, and cousins. But unlike my mother's family, who was led by an immigrant, my father's family has been entrenched in America for generations. The family, as I stated earlier, was, and still is, primarily located in southern Indiana. Specifically, the small town of Linton, which is where my father was born. The hospital where my father was born was the birthplace of generations of Linton residences, and was torn down to make way for a Wendy's restaurant. This is what led my father, and many other Lintonians, to tell you they were "born at Wendy's." I sure hope they had a sneeze guard in place at the salad bar. Linton is a small coal mining town in the heart of Greene County Indiana. It is a picturesque vision of Americana in its purest form. Its Main Street looks like the cover of an edition of The Saturday Evening Post. Small mom and pop shops dot the downtown area and many porches have American flags on them all year, not just on the Fourth of July. Everyone knows your name, and people still leave their doors unlocked. It is just a classic small American town.

Dad was one of three children had by Garry and Pansy Powell. My grandparents weren't the most affectionate people you'd ever meet. In fact, they were rather cold. I don't have a single memory of either of them telling anyone that they loved them. I'm sure they did, I just don't have any memories of it. It's just who they were. Grandpa was driven by two things...money and loyalty. Without either, there really was no place for you in his world. He was a WWII Naval Veteran who was involved in the D-Day invasion, and also served a tour in the Pacific near the Philippines. He was a larger than life presence in town with his unmistakable blue Chevy Suburban.

He was one of three partners in a machine shop in Chicago after the war. I don't have any memories of Grandpa and Grandma living in Chicago. I only have memories of him living in Linton, on an absolutely beautiful thirty-three-acre farm. He had the house built after my grandmother's health problems caused him to retire and settle back into his home town. The house was a three-bedroom, custom built brick ranch set about four hundred feet off the road. A white picket fence ran the entire length of the road in front of the property and the driveway was a long, sweeping blacktop with a landscaped island in the middle of it. In the summertime, the grandkids would be tasked with stripping and repainting that picket fence…a task I dreaded every year. Re-finishing that fence seemed like it took two years to complete, and it always felt like it was a thousand degrees out every day we worked on it. I wanted to burn that fence down on more than one occasion.

Grandpa always emphasized the importance of education, and he offered fifty dollars for every A you received on your report card throughout your high school career. Needless to say, I never once collected on that offer. On the other hand, my cousin, Leslie, received straight A's on every report card, so she cleaned up year after year. Grandpa hosted all night poker games in the back room of the house, where all his friends would gather to gamble, smoke cigarettes, and tell stories until the sun came up. Grandpa would have a brown paper grocery bag on the floor between his feet and, as the host of the event, he took one dollar from every pot as his cut. That paper grocery bag would be half full of one-dollar bills by morning. As a child, the amount of money that was sitting in any given pot on that poker table seemed like a million dollars to me. I was amazed at how much these guys could just afford to gamble away.

The back portion of Grandma and Grandpa's property was a pasture with a barn that Grandpa rented out to locals who needed grazing land. When I was a boy, cows were what were housed in that area. I specifically remember one year when the man renting the pasture brought in some new cows, and one bull. It was a Spanish bull named Mikey who had curved horns like a ram. Mikey was an absolute asshole of a bull. He was mean, territorial, and would often escape. Grandpa would have us come with him to the barn every morning during our summer stays to have us feed and water the cows. It was a messy, stinky task, but also kind of fun to watch the cows come herding in because they saw you enter the barn at feeding time.

I can still see Grandpa on his riding mower, spending hours cutting the grass. In the evenings, he would frequently fall asleep in his favorite chair with his oxygen mask on in front of the massive, all stone fireplace that was the focal point of the main living room. He chewed Skoal tobacco in the pouches, and there was a spit cup on almost every table in the house. When he wanted to enjoy some fresh air, he would sit on a swing bench off the side of the house and just enjoy the country breeze. He is, by far, where most of my genetic makeup originated. All Powell men look alike. ALL Powell men. I am a spitting image of my father, who was a spitting image of his father. And my son is now a spitting image of me. It's unkillable super DNA. I wonder if we will be immune when the zombie apocalypse breaks out due to our super DNA. Hmmm.

Grandma was a housewife and homemaker. She had suffered from a brain tumor in the late seventies, causing her to be partially paralyzed on one side of her body. One of her eyes would not make tears naturally, so my grandfather would apply drops to her eye, and then re-cover the eye with a see-through patch which was then taped to her skin to hold it in place. This had to be done several times a day. I would get the willies every time he changed her eye patch. Because of her condition, she walked with a cane and needed to be helped wherever she went. Through all of that, she managed to run a pretty tight household. The place was immaculate. Shoes were never allowed to be worn in the house. Ever. That was, by far, the biggest no-no in Grandma's world. To call Grandma a clean freak would be an insult to clean freaks everywhere. You weren't allowed to clean her floor with a mop. It had to be on your hand and knees with a rag and a bucket...and you damn well better get up in those corners. Her house was one step away from living in a museum, but with country decor.

Grandma's simple pleasures were playing gin with the ladies and visiting the beauty parlor to have her hair done. Her pride and joy was their dog, Maggie. Maggie was a small, black and white border collie who would snip at my hands ever since I tugged on her tail as a puppy. That dog hated me. I can't say that the feeling wasn't mutual, but I could never say that to Grandma. Hell no. She loved that dog so much, that she had an oil painting done of her after she passed, that hung in the living room. THEN, they bought an identical dog, and named it Maggie as well. Freaky.

Grandma's style of cooking was definitely southern comfort food. There was a lot of bacon and eggs, biscuits and gravy, and chicken and noodles. The kind of food that sits heavy in your gut after you're done eating. The kind of food you eat to keep your strength up to be able to work on a farm. After being forced to eat biscuits and gravy for so many years of my childhood, I can barely smell it now without having my gag reflex go into hyperdrive. I just can't eat that kind of heavy, gravy laden food anymore. And the taste of biscuits and gravy turns my stomach. I will never eat that dish again.

In addition to my father, Grandma and Grandpa had two other children...one of which was my Uncle Garry "Jake" Powell. Uncle Jake was my hero growing up. When I was just knee high to a grasshopper, he owned and operated Bailey Automotive Shop in Linton. It sat where the Subway in town now resides. It seems as if a lot of my father's family historical sites have been demolished to make way for a fast food joint. I can remember playing around in the shop for hours, watching him run the store and watching customers be scared out of their minds when Uncle Jake's Doberman Pinscher, Shade, would pop up from behind the counter. She was, to say the least, an intimidating presence, and always kept a watchful eye on the shop. Uncle Jake and Aunt Alona lived in Linton as well, in a beautiful stone home that I would marvel at every time I would visit. Prior to the stone house, they had a larger ranch home on several acres of land out in the country. I have a few memories of that house, but not many.

One of the most vivid memories from that larger country place is when we were all sitting around, shooting the breeze, under Uncle Jake's giant shade tree. My grandfather, as he would often do, was sitting on the riding lawn mower right up against the base of the tree. I guess nobody was really paying attention, because at some point my uncle had disappeared from the conversation. Then, out of nowhere, a loud shotgun blast rattled through the air and sent everyone heading for the ground. My uncle had gone into the house and retrieved a shotgun to shoot the rather large snake out of the tree that was perched just above my grandfather's head. The dead snake came falling out of the tree, landing on the riding mower my grandfather was sitting on. It scared the shit out of everyone. I was just a little boy, no older than my son is now, but at the time it seemed to me that the snake had to be at least fifty feet long. It was massive. Uncle Jake dragged it to the pond and tossed the dead carcass into the water. I'll never forget that moment as long as I live. And what is with my uncles and shotguns?

Uncle Jake would eventually become riddled with illnesses and impairments. Among the laundry list of health problems was the fact he eventually went completely blind. This was difficult for a man who would once race dragsters up and down the country roads. This once proud, independent man was now completely
dependent on others to survive. That was extraordinarily difficult to handle for him. But, as he did with everything, he figured out a "Jake system" for

overcoming every obstacle. He learned, before it was even a common practice, how to self-administer home dialysis...while completely blind...and did this multiple times a day. That poor man spent so many years of his life attached to some sort of medical device. That's just not fair to anyone.

Even though his body was rapidly failing, his mind was sharp as a tack. He would still sit in on the poker games my grandfather hosted in that back room, and my aunt would sit over his shoulder and whisper in his ear what his cards were, and what everyone else had on the table, and he could keep it all straight without having the ability to see it. The man designed and helped build a new shed, while completely blind. The word "handicapped" simply didn't apply to him. And he could always be counted on for an awesome quip. While out to dinner one night, the waitress hadn't noticed he was blind, and he could sense it as she went around the table taking everyone's order. When she came to Uncle Jake, she asked him what he would like, and he popped out his glass eye and said, "I don't know...let me have a look." He then held the eye up to the menu and moved it back and forth as if he was reading it through that eye. I've never seen a woman turn that white in my entire life. But the poor woman kept coming up behind him during dinner, forgetting he was blind. He would jump every time she startled him. After having come up behind him one too many times, she did it again and Uncle Jake slammed his hand down on the table and said, "Suck me off with a breast pump! You have to stop sneaking up behind me, woman!" She approached from the other side of the table for the rest of the dinner.

Uncle Jake's smile was infectious, and his laugh was unmistakable. Believe it or not, he was the one who taught me to drive. Yes...a completely blind man taught me to operate a vehicle on the gravel roads north of Linton. Because he was a larger than life figure in a very small town, he knew almost everyone, and almost everyone knew him. When I went to take my driver's license test at the state facility in town, it was my uncle who went with me. He and the person working behind the counter were friends and used to like to freak people out who were in the waiting area by having my uncle make his way up to the vision testing machine, tapping his guide cane along the way. He would then place his eyes into the machine and begin raising hands in a random pattern, seeming to indicate he was signaling when he saw the flashes from the test. The person working behind the counter would then inform him that he had passed, and would issue him his renewed license, to the shock and dismay of the people waiting to be tested next. And yes, he did have an actual valid driver's license from the state of Indiana because of his friendships. It's good to know people. Everyone needs a guy.

33

Another unusual, but unique story involving Uncle Jake was the time he and another uncle, Newt, went to Bloomington, Indiana to see Jake's doctors. Jake was completely blind, and Newt was blind in one eye, but still drove. As they left the doctor's office, Uncle Newt was attempting to turn left, and asked Uncle Jake how the oncoming traffic looked. Yes, I know, he asked a blind man if any cars were coming. In his defense, it was very shortly after Uncle Jake had lost his sight. Regardless, he would soon learn that he asked the biggest smart ass on the planet to put his full smart assedness on display. Being the jokester that he was, Uncle Jake swung his head around as if to look at the oncoming traffic and blurted out "Looks good to me!" Before Uncle Newt could ascertain that Jake was joking, he began to pull out and BAM...they got hit by an oncoming car. And did that stop Uncle Jake from being a smart ass? Hell no. After the crash had settled itself out, he declared to Uncle Newt "Well...it's a good thing we're close to a doctor's office!" Uncle Jake...a smartass until the very end.

Uncle Jake and Aunt Alona would eventually move from the stone house into a home immediately next door to my grandfather. This house is the one that I remember the best. They had another Doberman, Rocky, who was fiercely protective of Uncle Jake. If you so much as put your hand on Uncle Jake's shoulder as he sat in his chair, you would find yourself on the wrong end of Rocky. The weirdest part about Rocky was that he would bark like a crazed animal if you were at the front door but would then let you in without attacking you...but when you went to leave, he barked like mad and would nip at your heels to prevent you from leaving.

It was in this house that Uncle Jake would eventually succumb to his various ailments and pass away one sad August morning in 1988. Rocky was practically tearing through the walls of the bedroom my aunt locked him in trying to get at the paramedics working on him. Uncle Jake would be laid to rest in Linton, and, many years later, Aunt Alona would later pass way after her own battles with illness. They were both very instrumental people in my life. Aunt Alona was a true southern girl. A beautiful woman with the presence of Jackie Kennedy. She was the rock behind my Uncle in his most desperate times, and she always stood by her man. And, man, could she can food with the best of them. That woman would put me to work shucking corn, literally by the pickup truck load, for her to freeze for the winter. Aunt Alona was "zombie apocalypse ready" before it was cool.

34

Aunt Alona tolerated quite a bit of nonsense and mischief from my cousin and me. One distinct memory of my aunt was the time I stayed with them briefly one summer. At that stage in my rebellious life, I was going commando daily. I didn't like wearing underwear. While Aunt Alona was doing laundry one day, she noticed that I didn't have any underwear in the hamper. She asked me about it and I told her that I had stopped wearing underwear almost a year before. It was a pearl clutching moment for my aunt. The look of horror on her face was amazing. She couldn't believe it. She also demanded I get in the car and proceeded to drive me to the store where she bought me underwear. If I was staying in her house, I was wearing underwear. One night, my cousin, Jr, and I went on a little drinking spree. We returned to his place, where I laid down on the floor at the foot of Jr's bed, while he attempted to pass out on the bed. Aunt Alona came in and smelled the beer immediately. She leaned over him and asked him if he had been drinking. He told her he only had two beers, but this wasn't Aunt Alona's first rodeo, and she knew he was lying. We were woken up by her vacuuming his room at 6:00 in the morning. Brutal.

Uncle Jake and Aunt Alona had two kids, Garry and Lisa. Yeah....you're starting to sense a pattern with the men's names in my father's family, aren't you? Almost all of us are either Garry or Tommy with the middle name Lee or Wayne. My little brother, Michael, and one cousin, Danny, are the two exceptions.My cousin Garry, or "Jr", as everyone knew him, was the person I spent most of my freshman year in high school with. He was well older than I was, but he lived to party, and I loved to attend parties, so we were a natural fit. Jr had a way about him...almost a "kavorka" like aura. Those of you who are Seinfeld fans will get that reference. The ladies in town loved him. His distinctive king cab, deep red Ford ranger pickup truck was unmistakable on Saturday night cruises through town. When that beauty rolled into the parking lot, you knew who was behind the wheel. Jr was the one who gave me my first hit of weed, and my first tab of acid. I was like his mini-me and he was like my mentor at that point in life.

The very first time I ever took acid, Jr had a plan. He gave me the tab and waited until I was feeling its effects. He then dropped me off with some friends, informed them of my condition, and told them to keep an eye on me until he returned. Literally the only thing I can remember about sitting with my friends that day was me staring at my friend's head and asking him if his head was always that big. Barry did have a large head, but I shouldn't have pointed it out. Jr came to retrieve me after about an hour, and then took me to one of his friends' houses. His friend was married and had a toddler son still walking around in diapers. When we arrived, I guess Jr had already filled him in on my state of mind because I remember his friend asking if they could mess with me, and Jr saying that's why he brought me there in the first place. These people had me convinced we were in LA, while there was actual snow outside the window on the ground, and that we were just waiting for our ride to take us to have lunch with Motley Crue. And if that wasn't bad enough, around the corner comes this toddler in his diaper. Since the boy couldn't speak, I naturally couldn't understand a word he was attempting to say. This led to Jr and his friends convincing me that the boy was actually the sixty-five-year-old, midget German immigrant father of Jr's friend's wife, and the reason I couldn't understand him was because he was speaking German to me. I swear to God I'm not making this up. Keep in mind, I'm on acid for the very first time while all this is happening. So, with that information in hand, I set out to attempt to communicate with this fine midget immigrant. For hours I attempted to work out a mutual language between us that we both could comprehend so we could converse. I was even offering him cigarettes. I was basically a piping hot, tripping balls mess at this point. I gotta tell ya...I've looked better.

That was tame, though. Jr's partying would often get way more out of hand than that. His parties are still talked about around Linton to this day. One party really got out of hand in a big way. It was held at my grandparent's farm while they were out of town. Given the fact that he had several acres to work with, Jr made sure to really do it up big. I'll bet over half the high school was there. They drank beer and smoked weed until everyone was good and wrecked. A group of rather intoxicated party goers took turns pushing each other around the property on grandpa's larger farm tractor. They destroyed that place. My grandfather had a decorative well that had a small stone statue figure of a little black boy sitting on the edge of the well. Someone grabbed that statue before the night was out, and he was found the next morning, hanging from the rafters of the barn. Those boys got rowdy and caused some serious damage. Jr's sister, Lisa, would ultimately get in more trouble than Jr did for that party, because my aunt and uncle told her she should have stopped him. Yeah, right! As if that party was going to be stopped. Lisa would've had a better chance of having lunch with Jimmy Hoffa than stopping that historic party from happening.

Jr could also play the guitar really well. He had a couple of different guitars he liked playing, but his pink paisley fender guitar was the crown jewel of his collection. I would sit in his room and listen to him riff away in amazement. He is the one who introduced me to Jimi Hendrix, Pink Floyd, and Stevie Ray Vaughan, among many others. I can't even begin to count how many hours

36

were spent hotboxing his bedroom while he jammed some Hendrix. If only he had put some effort behind it, Jr could've been a great guitarist. For those reading this that don't know what "hotboxing" is, it is when you and some friends get together to smoke weed and you do it in a small, completely sealed room or structure, as to keep all of the smoke inside with you. We hotboxed that bedroom so many times you could scrape the resin off the walls.

After Uncle Jake passed, Jr was lost. He didn't know what to do with himself and his life. He was so close to his father, and now he was gone. In his quest to fill the void, he found himself enlisting in the Navy. Personally, I was shocked when he enlisted. After all, I had been there through his rowdiest partying and I just didn't see why he would want to have orders shouted at him, but he enlisted nonetheless. He would serve his tour of duty on the east coast and would frequently travel back to visit his family in Indiana. It was during these travels that he met Sharon, the woman who would eventually become his wife. Throughout their marriage, they were heavily involved in their church, and would frequently make trips from where they lived in Kentucky, back to see his mom and step-father, Howard.

Jr's job had him traveling quite a bit, and he would, from time to time, call me from the road to argue politics and talk sports. He was a conservative and I am a liberal, so our conversations would get heated sometimes, but always ended well. On January 21st, 2016, Jr called me from New Jersey to argue a little politics. Before we ended the call, he told me he would be in Chicago the following afternoon and wanted to know if I was available for lunch. I said we would see when tomorrow came and told him I would talk to him the next day. Shortly after I woke up the next morning, I got a call from my cousin, Lisa. She asked me if I was sitting down. My heart sank as my thoughts immediately raced to my Aunt Alona, whose health had been deteriorating. That's when she hit me with the news that Jr had died. I said that was impossible and that I was waiting for his call when he landed. But he wasn't coming. He had a heart attack while on the highway, and while speaking to his wife. He hung up the phone with her after telling her he needed to let her go. He then pulled off to the side of the road and died from his attack. He was just forty-nine years old. It rocked me. I was in stunned disbelief. He died young just like his father. I literally needed a moment to comprehend what had just happened. He and I had done so much together. We were like brothers. It was one of the most stunning pieces of news I had ever been told. But nobody was more stunned than Jr's sister, Lisa.

Lisa is the cousin that I have remained closest with from Dad's side of the family. Lisa didn't party like we did, although she sometimes got blamed for the aftermath of one of our benders, as was the case with the big blow out at my grandfather's place I mentioned earlier. Even though it was her brother I hung around with more in my youth, she has become like a sister to me, and right now we are just clinging to what's left of the once large, proud family we had. Lisa lives in Vicksburg, Indiana with her husband, Brad, and close to their children and grandchildren. While Jr was the rebel of their family, Lisa was the picture of success. She did well in school, played in the marching band, and never got in any trouble. She was the good girl of the family.

Right out of high school, she married Brad. I remember Brad coming over to my uncle's house and playing some of the most beautiful music I've ever heard on his acoustic guitar. Man…. Brad really could play the hell out of that guitar. I could listen to him play and just get lost in the melody. My Uncle Jake once asked him why he would ever keep playing that damn electric guitar when he makes such beautiful music on the acoustic guitar. My uncle also took full advantage of Brad's courtship of my cousin. When Brad came to ask my uncle permission to marry Lisa, Uncle Jake said to him "I don't know, Brad…a girl like that would fetch at least two cows in India." After a little bit of playful negotiating, they agreed that Brad's dowry to my uncle would be two Big Macs from the McDonald's in Sullivan, Indiana. At the time, it was the closest McDonald's, and it was far away, so my uncle rarely had the opportunity to eat a Big Mac. Brad made the journey to the Golden Arches, retrieved the two Big Macs, and delivered them as requested. He then received my uncle's blessing to marry his only daughter. The olden days… when people sold their daughters for meat.

Of everyone in the family, Lisa has taken more than her share of gut punches from life. She has lost her father, her mother, her only brother, as well as several aunts, uncles, cousins and all her grandparents. It has not been easy for her in the least bit. But
through everything life has thrown at her, she has persevered. She just keeps going like the Energizer Bunny. She and Brad had two children, Amber and Corey, who refer to me as "Uncle Tommy". Amber is pretty much exactly like her mother…determined, family oriented, and completely unwilling to tolerate anyone's bullshit. Cross Amber, and you WILL know it. She resides in Bruceville, Indiana with her husband, Tim, and their two sons, Cooper and Eli. We have the occasion to get together with them usually once a year these days, and usually when we make our annual pilgrimage to Holiday World in Santa Claus, Indiana. I absolutely love hanging out with those boys. They are

the sweetest kids you'll ever meet, but when they get going, it's like a Tasmanian Devil, inside a tornado, hopped up on Mt Dew. I will just say this…Amber may have her hands full with those boys once they hit their teens. And I will be right there, every step of the way, encouraging those boys. I predict my niece is going to give me some serious tongue lashings as the years progress.

Cory is a spitting image of his father. I like spending time with Cory, if we can just get him to stop rooting for the damn Lakers. I've had the privilege of watching Cory transform from a shy little country boy, to the stand-up man and husband he is today. Cory and his wife, Katie, live in Jasonville, Indiana, and have remained close with their parents. Katie is quiet, reserved, and so sweet she'll rot your teeth. Cory, if you're reading this, please know that you got lucky with that woman. One funny story of mine comes from Cory and Katie's wedding. As with all the weddings, Renee and I were in attendance. I was wearing my three-piece suit, fedora, and overcoat. Because of where we live, I have, what seems to them, is a very thick, Italian style, Chicago accent. I wouldn't know for some time after the wedding, but I apparently made an impression on Katie's little brother, who had asked her if I was in the mafia. Looking back on it, I can understand why he would think that. After all, I looked, and talked, like a wise guy straight from a gangster movie. Perhaps I have more in common with my grandfather than I assumed. Hey…fuhgettaboutit!

I had one blood aunt on my father's side, Bertha, who had three children of her own. When I was very little, Bertha and her first husband lived in a house right next door to my grandparents' house. It was a large, old house with great country charm. Her oldest daughter, Kim, was her wild child and would always be sneaking out in the middle of the night to go to a party. One night, Aunt Bertha put a kiddie pool filled with ice water under her bedroom window which Kim fell into trying to sneak out. I was over at their house watching cartoons one early Saturday morning when Kim came quietly creeping into the back door. My cousin, D.J., and I were in that back section of the house and watched her make her careful entrance. As she entered the kitchen, and then turned to head down the hallway to her bedroom, she was met by Aunt Bertha who proceeded to whack her in the head with a tennis racket. D.J. and I let out a hell of a laugh, and then promptly shut up as Aunt Bertha turned to look at us. As soon as we went silent, she told us to continue to laugh because she wanted everyone to see what she was about to do. She must've whacked Kim with that tennis racket twenty times as they made their way down that hallway.

Bertha was away and out of the picture for a very long time, until my grandparents became ill at the tail end of their life. That's when she returned to play the part of the sympathetic daughter who wanted to help. What she was really doing was putting it into my grandparents' heads that she was the only one who really cared about them and telling them that if my father cared about them, he would move back from Chicago to help take care of them. My grandfather was the first to pass away, followed by my grandmother a couple years later. When we attended my grandmother's funeral, my father wasn't feeling well and wanted to go back to the house to lie down. Bertha made sure her daughter's husband escorted my father back to the house and then made him stay there while Dad napped. They were afraid he was going to steal something. Here was my father, attending his mother's funeral, being treated like a criminal by his own family. What an asshole move on their part. But it would pale in comparison to what came next. It turned out that Bertha was so good at persuading my grandparents of her lies, that she got them to change their will, and cut Dad out completely. He got nothing. He got no personal belongings from either of his parents, no mementoes of any kids, and Bertha got all the money and the house. It was an evil move and I hope she is haunted by it for the rest of her miserable life. I have long since left Bertha where she belongs…at the curb with the rest of the garbage.

It's funny how a family can splinter. My father's family once had massive family reunions where family members from as far away as Indianapolis, Kentucky, and California would come in. There would be so many of us, that my grandfather's 380-foot-long driveway would be filled with cars. We would have a softball game, eat until we burst, and stay up into the wee hours of the morning swapping stories and telling lies. Now all that remains are fragmented sections of the family scattered across the county. It's a damn shame the way it falls apart like that. Don't do that with your family. It is damn near impossible to get back.

Tom Powell Jr.

"CHILDREN LEARN MORE FROM WHAT YOU ARE THAN WHAT YOU TEACH." – W.E.B. DUBOIS

CHAPTER FOUR
The unlikely parents of a legend

Now that I've laid some of the ancestral foundation of my large family, I'd like to take a moment to tell you about my parents themselves. Before you read any further, please be advised that I am telling the story of my life with as much brutal honesty and vivid detail as I can, and this chapter will mark the beginning of some dark tales. That being said, each and every one of these true stories contributed to making me who I am today, so I must accept them as building blocks in my house of life.

My parents were very imperfect people trapped in a very imperfect marriage. I understand that everybody's parents were imperfect, but as I mentioned in the preface, mine took it to a level not many people's parents take it to. Let's start with my father, Tommy Lee Powell Sr. Dad was a hot shot running around the streets of Chicago and was professionally racing dragsters in his late teens and early twenties. He and my Uncle Jake would often roll the race car out of the garage and down the street before starting it as not to alert my grandparents that they were heading out racing again. He didn't want to settle down. He didn't want a family. He wanted to keep living the party life. As I mentioned earlier, he ran dragsters from US 30 to Oswego to the Rt 66 strip. He mainly raced dodge cars that bore names such as "Powell's Demon," "Juniors Toy," and "The Fugitive." Uncle Jake served as his crew chief and Grandpa financed the whole operation through the original Powell Enterprises, and his Chicago based machine shop, Blanchard Grinding. They were getting their blowers from Gary Dyer, and his shop, Dyers Superchargers, based out of Stickney, Illinois. For the Powell Boys, life was a party. But, one day, Tom met a young girl working at the Cock Robin that once sat in the parking lot of Gene & Jude's Hot Dogs, and his life would change forever. Since he was addicted to Gene & Jude's hot dogs, and he always maintained a ravenous sweet tooth, he would often get his hot dogs, eat them in the car, and then hit the Cock Robin for a little ice cream. He saw what he thought was a cute young Italian girl working there, so he would always request it be her that make his ice cream. I guess that was his weird way of flirting…making a woman prepare some type of food for him. Dad was perpetually stuck in 1952. After several visits for his sweet tooth craving, he finally asked her out. A one-night stand later, and he was preparing to welcome a son into the world. He would soon become a slave to his situation, as tends to happen to the unprepared.

Dad was a solid guy and always provided for his family, but he did so to a fault. He was basically never around for most of my childhood. He worked a full-time day job, a part time night job, and worked at a garage on half the weekends, so his whole life was spent working. And when he wasn't working on the weekend, he was at the track. I understand why he worked so much, I just wish he was around a little more. But when he was around, I was attached to him at the hip. I idolized that man when I was a child. The old man never raised a hand against us, always provided for us, and I believe he truly cared for his family. I say it in that manner because, believe it or not, the man never told me he loved me. Not one time that I can recall. He's told me he was proud of me for one thing or another and had occasionally given me the man-to-man approval pat on the back, but never told me he loved me. I never mentioned it to him, because I wanted him to say it without being prompted, but he went to his last breath without saying it. Of everything about my father, that is the one thing I wish I could go back in time and change. It's the biggest reason why I say it to my kids all the time. Folks...if you have children, tell them you love them daily. You have no idea how corrosive it is to never hear your father say it. As I write this, I am forty-five years old, my father has been dead for two and a half years, and it still eats at me. Don't do that to your kids. My father's way of telling you he loved you was giving you money for things you needed or wanted. While I hated that aspect of him, I understand why he was the way he was given how he was raised.

Because he worked so much, he would sometimes miss holidays. I can remember refusing to eat Thanksgiving dinner at my aunt's house until Dad arrived. I sat on the couch in the living room, starting out the window as I waited to see his car coming down the street...but he never came. It would be yet another holiday without my father. My mother never understood why I continued to cling to a man that was never around, but he was my father. I was a child. What did she expect? She just wanted everyone to hate who she hated. Sorry, Ethel, but that's not how this works.

Dad usually could be found with his pipe in hand. The smell of Middleton's Cherry Blend pipe tobacco hung in the house so heavily, our clothes smelled like it. I miss that smell. In our house, there was always an ashtray full of used pipe tobacco and an allen wrench, which was Dad's tool of choice for digging the old tobacco out of his pipe. The end of his right thumb was permanently charred from using it to tamp down the tobacco after taking a drag. I cannot even begin to calculate how many dollars I have spent on cherry blend tobacco for Dad over my lifetime.

He wasn't exactly what you would call an expert on fine dining either. In fact, most of what he ate would make a billy goat puke. One of his favorite snacks to make during a football game or televised drag racing event was fried egg sandwiches. He would toast an entire loaf of bread and fry a dozen eggs. He would then make fried egg sandwiches out of all of that, with ketchup on each sandwich. Then he would have a cereal bowl filled with syrup, and he would dip the sandwiches into the syrup before eating them. I know...you're trying to re-read that last sentence to make sure you read it correctly, aren't you? Yeah, you read it correctly. Hopefully none of you reading this have recently eaten. His taste in food was horrendous. He loved pepper and egg

45

sandwiches on Fridays during lent, which is not unusual at all, but he would have his dipped in the beef juice the same way you dip your Italian beef sandwich. Vile. Disgusting. Putrid. He would frequently stop for a Maxwell Street polish with onions and mustard and cause the car to stink of onions and polish sausage for three days. And always with the hot dogs. The man would kill his best friend for a Gene & Jude's hot dog. If he was ever on death row, his last meal would be two Gene & Jude's hot dogs and a Dr Pepper.

Dad was a large man who always had facial hair. Usually a goatee, but occasionally a full beard. His hands were permanently stained from working in the machine shop. The ends of his fingers were stained black and showed the various cuts and scrapes he endured on a weekly basis. He wasn't posing for the cover of GQ anytime soon. He was a good old boy with southern roots, and he wasn't what Mom wanted in a husband. He drank and smoked, he liked to hang out with the guys, and, most of all, he wasn't Italian. What Mom always wanted was what her sister always had. She wanted a nice house in a cul-de-sac, with a nice white-collar husband, and a couple kids playing in the yard. What she got was a blue collar, good old boy who raced cars and worked in a machine shop. If she could ever just see past the fact that he came home from work dirty instead of carrying a briefcase, she might have seen that she had a pretty solid guy. He wasn't running around on her, always provided for the family, and was about as down to earth as you were going to find. Sure, he had his tendencies that drove her nuts, as all spouses have, but she wasn't winning any personality awards either. Trust me.

My mother was the opposite of Dad. She did tell me she loved me and did so frequently. The difference between her and Dad, though, was her actions didn't match her words. I was constantly shunned by my mother in favor of my brother. I believe it was because I was a stark reminder of a life gone awry. I was a spitting image of the man who got her pregnant and ended any dreams she had in life. I carried his name and looked exactly like him. Even worse, I idolized him, while she despised him. Everything about me reminded her of the life she was handed, over the life she wanted. She was just sixteen when she became pregnant with me. My father was in his mid-twenties. This wasn't what she had planned at all. She had me just weeks before her seventeenth birthday. One day she's in high school, with her whole life ahead of her, and the next day she's a seventeen-year-old mother of one with a husband and a mortgage. Life comes at you fast. So, with her new, unwanted life, and a daily reminder of why she was in the situation she found herself drowning in, I became her target. I became the release valve for her anger and rage. I became her punching bag.

46

Mom was a large, hulking woman. She had enormous feet. No...I don't mean she had "big" feet...I mean she had freakishly gigantic feet. The woman had some feet on her feet. And she had huge man hands that were bigger than my father's. She was tall, with broad shoulders, and a very square frame. She was the kind of woman that reminded you of the wife of a Russian beet farmer. When she stood with her arms at her side, the tips of her hands went far lower than most people's hands would. She was just an extremely unattractive woman. She looked like she should be on a roller derby squad in the seventies. I often joked with Dad later in life that he actually caught a Bigfoot, shaved it, taught it to speak, and then married it. She might have been a looker in her teens, but if that was true, she sure as hell lost it somewhere along the way.

Mom hated working. She wanted to be the stay at home mom who spent her days running kids to practice and watching soap operas. She had the "Keeping Up With the Kardashians" mentality way before its time. The woman constantly complained about every job she ever held. Because she wasn't skilled in anything, and had no formal education of any kind, she worked as a laborer in numerous different factory positions. She was always tired and constantly miserable. She would come home every bit as dirty as my father and she hated every last second of it. One job, at Elkay, broke her back so much, she quit within days of starting it. She's literally did everything from sweeping floors, to sanding metal sink basins, to putting together pinball machines during my childhood.

Her cooking style can best be described as "white trash poor chic." Our mashed potatoes came from a box and our burgers were never store bought. Regular white bread often served as not only sandwich bread, but also hamburger and hot dog buns. When she made her meatloaf, she would always put a hard-boiled egg in the center of it, so you would get a slice of egg in the center of your piece of meatloaf. I despised that woman's cooking. I still don't comprehend how she came from a family of great Italian cooking yet would consistently fuck up the simplest of meals. She thought miracle whip was better than real mayonnaise, so that's what we had on our sandwiches. Have you ever eaten a bologna sandwich on wonder bread with miracle whip and relish? That was a staple for me as a youngster. Its vile, disgusting food that isn't suitable for prisoners.

Mom was very close to her family and leaned on them a lot throughout the years. She never really cared for my father's side of the family and would always complain whenever we made the trip down to see my grandparents. She always said that Indiana was the flattest, most boring state in the county and it should be wiped off the face of the earth. Every time she would make the trip South with us she would be more miserable than the last trip. She did have a good connection with some of my father's family in Southern California, and actually stayed in touch with their kids over the years. She also had a fondness for my father's cousin, Merle Gene, and was caught trying to make out with him one year at the family reunion. The woman was a tramp from day one. Who tries to hook up with their husband's cousin at the family reunion? I mean, come on. Mom was a constant embarrassment to our family.

The result of this unholy union between two unwilling participants, shockingly, was a divorce. Tom and Ethel had one more child, a boy, named Michael, but not even two young children at home was incentive enough for them to work it out. It was just never going to work. The only thing Tom and Ethel had in common was a night of steamy backseat sex. That's it. They hated each other outside of that setting. And that, boys and girls, is your life lesson from this chapter…keep your legs closed and your dick in your pants because one night's worth of passin' the gravy may not be worth completely altering your whole life over. The fact that Mom was having an affair with their accountant, Sylvester, didn't help matters much either.

So, being the evil, manipulative bitch she was, my mother got my father drunk one night and had him sign some "insurance papers". They were actually divorce papers she had drawn up ahead of time, behind my father's back. And, as you can imagine, the divorce agreement my father unwittingly signed favored her in the split. My father passed out, and my mother loaded me and my brother into the car and we headed to my Aunt Minah and Uncle Ken's house in Ohio. I didn't know what had happened because I was too young, and Mom wouldn't have told me anyway. I didn't think anything of the fact that Dad wasn't making the trip with us, because he had missed several trips in the past. All I knew was I was going to get to visit my cousins, Mineka and Joy, and at that age, that's all that really mattered in life.

When my father awoke from his drunken stupor the next morning, he found himself on the front lawn with all his clothes next to him, the locks on the house had been changed, and a copy of the divorce papers he signed was attached to the front door. The divorce agreement gave Mom everything in the bank account, the house, and full custody of my brother and me. She had suckered him. Took him for what little he was worth. It was a shitty move. A

48

bitch move. An Ethel move. My father had to go to court to fight for the every other weekend visits he would eventually be awarded. She wouldn't even give him that without a fight. Ethel was a vindictive woman with a streak of pure evil that ran right down the center of her cold, dead spine. She was ruthless. The two of them were the worst thing that ever happened to each other. I'm actually surprised it lasted eight years. I don't know how he tolerated that woman for that long.

After the divorce, my brother and I lived with my mom while Dad lived out of suitcases in friends' basements. We continued our daily routine almost as if nothing happened, except now Sylvester was around a lot more. Suddenly Sylvester was attending family parties with us. It all became very odd to me. I began to grow closer with my father, even though my chances to see him grew more and more rare, while my brother began to bond far more with our mother. I kept waiting for my parents to get back together like a naive fool, not realizing at the time that it was irreconcilable. Things just weren't the same. This wasn't how it was supposed to be. I was officially a child of divorced parents. I wasn't happy about the situation at all.

To be honest, they never should've married one another. The best thing that could've happened to either one of them is if they had just terminated the pregnancy and gone their separate ways. The hell and anguish they unleashed on themselves, and everyone around them, was massive. I don't think I could hand pick two people more wrong for each other than Tom Powell and Ethel LaFiura. What a disaster.

This period of living with Mom, while Dad was no longer in the picture, saw Mom begin to play herself off as some kind of modern day super woman. I distinctly remember her crying tears of joy and hugging me in celebration after she fixed a drawer handle in the kitchen one day. She was so elated because she had proven she didn't need a man to help her survive in life, and she was showing it now that she had thrown Dad out. Calm down, Ethel. It was a friggin' drawer handle. I mean, if she was seriously that unprepared about the simplest of basic household tasks, it's no wonder she was a complete failure as a mother. I remember Mom bragging to people about how she was "doing it on her own." No, you weren't. Look…everybody needs help sometimes, including me, and I am all for taking advantage of the help provided, but then don't go around bragging about how you're standing on your own two feet. You aren't. Mom was receiving child support (when Dad actually did send it), had 100% free day care from her mother, and was receiving government assistance. Our refrigerator and pantry always had government issued staples. My sandwiches had government cheese on them. So yeah, I was pissed at her. She threw Dad out. She upset the apple cart. She has now introduced this new man into our lives. She turned everything upside down. I don't know why she didn't just take my uncles up on the offer and get herself out of it all. She ruined so many lives in this process, it's stunning.

Tom Powell Jr.

"YOU THINK ABOUT CHILD ABUSE AND YOU
THINK OF A FATHER VICIOUSLY ATTACKING
A DAUGHTER OR A SON, BUT IN MY CASE IT
WAS MY MOTHER. MY MOTHER, I WOULD
SAY, WAS A...VERY BRUTAL DISCIPLINARIAN."
– LYNN JOHNSTON

CHAPTER FIVE
The kid who "fell"

I'm just going to lay it out as plainly as I possibly can...my mother beat me on a regular basis. I was the kid who always "fell" ...or at least that was the frequent excuse that was given to explain away my various bruises and welts. And when I say I was beaten, I am not talking about a spanking or a swift smack on the ass. I'm talking about beatings. I suffered punishment with belts, shoes, and anything else my mother could find to hit me with. I was hit with
open hand slaps and closed fists. I was welted, scarred and bruised a lot of my childhood. When I would get to visit my father every other weekend, he would take polaroids of my bruises and scars that he kept for later usage.

Many times, I thought about hitting my mother back, but never did. I just took it. I took every lash of every belt swing. I took every shoe sole to my backside. I took the slaps in the face and the punches in my back. I took it all. I took it because I didn't know how to respond to it, and because I just hoped it would stop one day. But it didn't. It just kept getting worse. My mother never seemed to get her fill of beating me, no matter what the offense. Bad grade? Beating. Messy room? Beating. It got to point where the only time I got any attention from her at all was when she was beating me.

My beatings would come for a variety of reasons. Sometimes it was my mother doing the hitting, and sometimes it was my soon to be step-father, Sylvester, who did the hitting. If I spoke back to either of them, I got hit. If I didn't clean the kitchen just right, I got hit. If I did bad in school, I got hit. It didn't matter the offense; the punishment was always physical. My mother never hit my brother...it was always me. I believe it was because, as I mentioned earlier, I reminded her of her ex-husband, and Michael did not. My mother denied ever laying a hand on me until the day she died, but she knew what she did. She knew the pain she inflicted. She was just too ashamed to ever admit it.

One time, I was beaten for dropping a gallon of milk. I would frequently be sent a few blocks away from our house to the local White Hen Pantry. Back in those days, my mother could hand me money and a note for anything, including cigarettes, and the store clerk would give me what I needed and send me back to my mother. Picking up a gallon of milk was a frequent errand I was tasked with. One day, when I was around ten, I was coming home from the White Hen when I dropped the gallon of milk. It didn't break open and spill, it was just dented on one side and a little dirty. I instantly knew I was going to get some type of beating for this. The rest of my ride home my heart was racing, and I was crying in anticipation of what kind of beating I was going to receive today. I was so terrified, that I stopped at the neighbors' house to try and hide. Our neighbor told me I had nothing to worry about and sent me home. Gloria was such a nice lady. Her husband was a gigantic man. Dave was a union bricklayer and had the kind of build that instantly made you realize you didn't want to get into a scrape with him. Their son, Dave Jr, was a metal head and had a piranha in a fish tank in his room. He dropped several quarters around the inside of the tank and dropped a silver dollar right where the piranha usually hung out. His friends would get high and see how much money they could retrieve from the tank before having their hand bitten. Upon entering the house, my mother saw my tears, and saw the milk, and just lost it. My punishment that day was to strip completely naked and lay down on the couch, belly down. My mother then had me put my arms over the arm of the couch, where she held them down tightly, so I couldn't move. Then Sylvester proceeded to beat my lower back and ass with a belt. I bled and couldn't sit down for hours. I screamed for him to stop, and screamed for my mother to make him stop, but he just continued beating me until he had his fill for the day. I can honestly tell you that Sylvester was one person I wish I had the opportunity to kill for what he did to me. I hated that man. The next day, when my mother learned I had stopped in to the neighbors to hide in fear, I received another beating. It seemed as though my mother would never get enough of beating me.

Earlier in this book I detailed the issue I had with my legs and the fact that had to wear leg braces as a child to correct the issue. One long lasting result of my leg issues as a child, even to this day, is that I will drift, while I walk, ever so slightly to my right side. One day, my mother, my brother, Sylvester and I were all heading into Brookfield Zoo. There is a north parking lot that has access to the main gate via an underground tunnel that passes under a busy road. While we were walking through this tunnel, I was slightly ahead of Sylvester and my mother and I began to drift to my right, which meant I was continuously walking in front of Sylvester. I was about twelve at this point, so I was a little bigger, and a little stronger. I also had several years of beatings under my belt and knew how to take a hit. Sylvester told me to stop waking in front of him, and I tried my very best not to, but once he said something, it was in my head. So, I kept drifting. After about the third time, he shoved me in the back and told me to stop it while calling me a dummy. I just kept walking. He would shove me again. I kept walking. Around the fifth time he

shoved me, I snapped. I spun around, grabbed him by the shirt, and slammed him against the wall of the tunnel. I didn't know if I could beat him in a fight, but at this point, I was ready to find out. It didn't take much to manhandle Sylvester as he was a short, nothing of a man. He was pathetic. I informed him that if he ever touched me again, I would kill him. My mother instantly jumped between the two of us and yelled at me to stop. When my attention turned to her, and was no longer focused on Sylvester, he took his shot. A right cross landing squarely on my chin that put me on my ass in a split second. But the thing was...I was older. I was stronger. I had taken enough beatings that one
punch didn't put me down for good. So, I popped right back up. But as soon as I had my legs under me once again, I sensed the tension in the air, and thought it would be best not to escalate things any further, so I simply walked back to the car, with the rest of family right behind me. I didn't give him the beat down he deserved that day, but I did show him that a right cross from an adult man wasn't enough to put me down, and I believe he knew it. I could see it in his face. He knew the tide had turned. Mom doled out the punishment herself from that day on. Sylvester was a true coward, only able to impose his dominance on a child, never someone who was a formidable match for him. If I could go back in time to that exact moment, I would beat that man to death in that tunnel.

One time, during a party my mother was hosting, I took all the kids in attendance around the house and showed them where all the mouse traps were located. My mother was utterly humiliated by this. Once everyone had left for the evening, I was called downstairs to talk to her. When I came down the stairs, my mother hit me in my back with a shoe. The sudden attack caused me to spin away from her, and I landed on the couch. As she came at me with the shoe once again, I cowered back and put my arms up to defend myself. All I could do was stay curled up on the couch and take each blow she landed. All you could hear throughout the house was the sound of shoe leather against my body and the sounds of my screams. After my beating was finished, I was instructed to return her shoe to the shoe area by the front door and go to bed. She was done for the night. Thankfully.

When I was in seventh grade in Addison, I hated the lunches my mother made, so I would stuff them in my locker and refuse to eat them. I don't know why I didn't just throw them away, but I didn't. Eventually, the stench from my locker drew attention from school officials. I never went to my locker for anything other than to stuff another sack lunch into it, so I didn't care. Needless to say, the school administrators wanted to have a chat with me, and subsequently, my mother. I knew that my mother would not be able to contain her anger when she learned of this, so I prepared for another beating. I was almost thirteen at this point and had broad shoulders and a strong back. If you wanted to hurt me, you had to try. When my mother learned of the days and days of wasted lunches in my locker, she grabbed me with her left arm while driving her right fist into my lower back and kidney area. That day was the most frustrated I have ever seen my mother, because I would not cry. I would not scream. I just absorbed each punch without emotion, until she was finished. And with each blow she landed, I envisioned punching her back, but I never did. Once again, I took it. I let her use me as her punching bag to release the anger of her life upon. She could beat my body, but she wasn't going to get the satisfaction of seeing me cry ever again. From that day forward, I never cried in front of my mother for anything ever again.

As soon as I turned thirteen, I ran away from my mother's home. In the state of Illinois, at that time, a child of thirteen or older could decide who they wanted to live with in a divorced family, so I made my choice. We were at Sylvester's condo in River Grove, which we were hanging out at more and more. Mom would park us in front of his TV in the living room while her and Sylvester would head to the bedroom for a little slap and tickle. I stood outside the condo, contemplating my move, literally for two hours. Then I just took off. I walked over forty-five minutes away, found a payphone, and called my father. He was remarried to a woman named Arlene at the time, and the two of them came and picked me up. My mother was furious. She vowed to fight my decision in court. She kept her rage and anger with her all the way to the courthouse, until my father's lawyer confronted her and her lawyer before entering the courtroom. My father had with him a shoe box full of polaroids of my bruised and beaten body. These were pictures from throughout my life, not just some recent incidents. I had also agreed to testify in court to the extent of her abuse. This was enough for her to sign over custody of me to my father, while she kept custody of my brother. This was effectively the nail in the coffin for my relationship with my brother. And while I wanted to still see my brother at that time, the fact that the beatings had ended was far more important to me. I never let anyone beat me again after I moved out of my mother's house. Nobody was going to ever treat me like a punching bag again without getting some of it in return. I was done being a doormat and ready to take control of my life.

Only one other time after that did any adult raise their hands to me. While living with my father and Arlene, Dad and I had a huge blow up. In the process of this blow up, my father snapped and threw me across the room.

He then grabbed a La Grange Park phone book and came after me with it. As he did so, Arlene was screaming for him to stop because on the abuse I suffered at my mother's hand. He didn't stop, and charged all the way across the room, where I stood, defiantly, waiting for him to swing. I told him he could swing that phone book at me, but once he did, I would knock him on his ass, no matter how many attempts it took me to accomplish that task. He saw me standing my ground, realized the situation, and never swung that phone book at me. He also never raised his hand to me again. As I said, I was done being anyone's punching bag. From now on, I was beating anyone's ass who laid a hand on me. Anyone.

The ultimate result of my childhood with my mother was a life in which we drifted in and out of each other's lives over the years. We would go years at a time without speaking, and then try to reconcile once again, only to see it fail. She never again raised a first to me, but she always denied ever hitting me. I honestly don't know how she could live with herself knowing what she did. And I could certainly never forget what she had done.

After my second child was born, my grandfather on my father's side passed away, and Renee thought I should call my mother to let her know, so she can let Michael know. If Michael chose not to do anything with that information, that was his choice, but she felt his actions shouldn't be influenced by me not letting them know. So, I made the call. During that call, Mom asked if she could see her grandchildren. I said yes, and this kicked off the last time my mother and I would try to reconcile.

In the beginning, we would see her, or speak to her on the phone, about once a month. She came to the parties for the girls and we saw hew around the holidays in a small get together usually just after the holidays had passed. She would occasionally take the girls for a weekend and was mildly involved in our lives. At first, I was apprehensive about leaving the girls alone with her after what she had done to me, but she ultimately never tried to hurt them like she did me. At least not physically. This continued until my brother had his first child. Once his first daughter was born, we saw, or spoke to, Mom about once every two to three months. The interactions were getting more and more sparse, and she would occasionally miss a family event. She was beginning to spend more time with Michael's kid and less time with mine. It was beginning again. Then my brother had his second child. After that, we saw, or spoke with, Mom about every six months, and her absence at family events became more frequent. I knew what was happening. I was back to being a second-class citizen again. I was used to it, but now it was affecting my kids. The topper came when both my brother and I had our third kids. When my third child was born, Mom made it to the hospital for a couple hours the day he was born, and we didn't see her again for over a month. When my brother's third child was born, Mom took the week off work and was at the hospital every day, all day, for the whole week. I was furious. But that's who Mom was. She was a manipulative bitch without a shred of decency in her body. To do that to me was one thing…she had a history of that…but to do that to my kids? No. You can go to hell.

My mother passed in January of 2017. She was found alone in her bed, surrounded by filth, by my brother, after nobody heard from her for a few days. I have long resented my mother for what she did to me and must admit that I didn't shed a tear upon hearing of her death. At the time, we weren't speaking to each other for the fourth time in our lives. She used my kids to feel like a grandmother just until Michael had kids of his own, at which point she discarded my kids like garbage. The following is my final message to her.

I will not grieve for you, because you don't deserve my grief. I will not mourn you, cry for you, or miss you. You were not just a horrible parent, but an evil human being. Who beats their child in the way you beat me? I'll tell you who…an evil person completely devoid of any human decency. You were the worst kind of person…you took your anger out on a child. You were evil. You served this earth no good, and only took from it what would've have been better used in a person with an ounce of humanity. The world is a better place now that you're no longer in it. While you didn't deserve to die peacefully in your sleep, I take solace in the fact that you at least died alone. If you were awakened by the medical attack that ended your life, my hope is that you experienced fear in your final moments. The kind of fear I felt every time you reached for the belt. The kind of fear I felt whenever I did the slightest thing wrong, and I knew another beating was heading my way. I hope you took that fear with you to the grave. And while I'm not a religious man, if there is a heaven and hell, then surely you are roasting in hell for all eternity for what you've done. You've earned every second of misery that comes your way. May you rot for all eternity.

If you are a victim of child abuse, or know someone who is, please call 800-422-4453. What you are living through is not normal, and there is help. You are not alone, and there are people who will help you.

If you are a parent who beats their child…stop. You are doing immeasurable damage. Your children are not there for you to take out your rage and frustration on. They are children. Stop what you are doing and seek help.

I specifically cut this chapter short as not to fill your heads with the many images of a child being beaten by their parent. I believe the examples I have laid out here are enough of an example of the horror I faced, and the evil that lived within my mother. Some members of my family will read this and deny it ever happened. To those in that camp, let me say this: You can deny it all you want, but we all know what happened. We all know what kind of woman Ethel was. I understand that family ties run deep, but not even family ties should prevent the truth from being told. Ethel Powell was a child abuser and should have had her children taken away from her. She had a mental disorder. She needed help.

"I THINK GROWING UP IN INDIANA PREPARES ANYONE FOR A LIFE IN COMEDY. I DO FEEL LIKE THERE IS A CERTAIN KIND OF SELF-EFFACING CYNICISM AMONG ALL HOOSIERS."
– JIM GAFFIGAN

CHAPTER SIX
A violent end, and a new beginning

As I stated earlier, my father had remarried by the time I decided I wanted to live with him. He was married to a woman named Arlene, who had two daughters and a son from a previous marriage. They got married in the living room of their home in La Grange Park, IL. It was a small, quick ceremony, in which I was the best man. The front living room had an open hallway above it that led to the master bedroom, and the wedding party was positioned along that overlook, with guests in chairs down below. I remember it being dimly lit, hot as hell, and I didn't know anyone there besides Dad. He had dated Arlene for a very short period and I didn't have a chance to meet her prior to the wedding. So here I am, with all the crap that's going on in my life, being introduced to my new step-mother for the first time, at her wedding, in which I'm the best man. Paging Jerry Springer. Mr. Springer, call for you on line two! So now, when I ran away from my mother's house, I became a part of this big mixed family, all thrust together without warning.

It was during this period of my life that I found myself attended S.E. Gross Jr High. A change of towns and schools as I began the repeat of the seventh-grade year I had failed at Indian Trail Junior High. Not only do I not know a single other student in the school, but I'm a full year older than all of them. Awesome. I would end up setting the record for most detentions by a seventh grader, and again by an eighth grader. Now that I think about it, I wonder if those records still stand today. Hmm. My gym teacher was a short, stout woman with an extremely noticeable mustache named Ms. Belcher. I remember once getting a detention because, as I was in the midst of an argument with Ms. Belcher, I said her name using a belching sound and then telling her to go shave that stash. She literally dragged me to the principal's office. I was such a little asshole. But I didn't care because at the time, Dad was once again working three jobs and, as was the case years **earlier** in my life, he wasn't around. Arlene didn't feel like she could discipline me in the beginning, so I had nobody riding my ass, so I became a rebellious little prick...again.

61

Another detention I received was when we were dissecting frogs. The teacher was growing aggravated with my antics in class that day, but I had the kids in the class laughing, so I kept going. I was the class clown in those days. I could get a laugh out of all the kids, and a good chunk of the teachers. As the teacher's frustration was reaching peak levels, I went into my headlining act for the day…I took a dead frog carcass, held it up as if it were standing, and proceeded to act out the old Looney Tunes bit with the singing frog. I would kick his legs up and down in a chorus line-like manner while singing "Hello my baby, hello my darling, hello my ragtime gal." And I did this as the teacher was standing at my desk, tearing me a new ass, while everyone in the room was trying to keep it together. That was the apparently the straw that broke the camel's back, and off to the principal's office I went. What did I say?

While attending S.E. Gross Jr High, I met some great friends…some of which I am still friends with today, even if some are only through social media. There was Kevin, who now resides in Florida and has some awesome hippie kids and a VW bus loving, bead wearin' hippie of a wife; Allen, who now has a wife and two kids in North Riverside; Becky who went on to become an actress; and many more such as John, Jimmy Janos, Ken, Jerry and a slew of others. I can honestly say I had fun with the friends I made in those days. We would play pick up football, go eat at Bills on 26th, and ride our bikes until our legs were about to fall off. The woods near my house provided great bike trails, and some off-road dirt trails, that we took advantage of daily. Man…do you remember riding your bike for hours on end without a cell phone or pager? You'd wind up two towns over and stop in at some random convenience store for a drink and some candy, and then ride all the way back home. Those were some great times.

We would have impromptu parties in my basement when my father and Arlene went grocery shopping. With such a large family, they would often have to buy quite a bit of groceries, and they would frequently go out to dinner beforehand to get a little alone time. That's when I discovered that there was plenty of time to have quick pop up parties at my place. Since we had limited time, we didn't waste any of it. As the host, I felt it was my duty to supply my guests with the necessary party favors, so I would raid Dad's stash of Amaretto, and we would all start chugging. I shall not name specific names in this particular story as it may embarrass some people, but during one such impromptu shindig, we heard my father's car way earlier than normal. Dad and Arlene had been jawing at each other all night and they skipped dinner, so they were home over an hour early. And here I was with several teenage kids in my basement bedroom, drinking my father's Amaretto. This wasn't going to end well. Party attendees quickly started making their way out the bedroom window as Dad and Arlene brought in groceries. The driveway and door were on one side of the house, and my bedroom was on the other side, so a bedroom window escape route was perfect…as long as it was executed properly. Because I was in a basement room, the window was high, and you crawled out onto the ground. Ok…let's go, people. Time's a wastin'. Move. Your. Asses. One by one they all made it out, until I was down to two of my guy friends that Dad knew were over, and one girl he didn't know was there. As she began to climb out the window, she got stuck. Shit! Frantically the three of us began shoving on her ass to try and get her out the window. It was at that moment that the bedroom door flew open. It was my father who had come downstairs to ask why I wasn't upstairs helping to bring in groceries. So, picture it, if you will…me and two of my friends trying to shove some girl out of my bedroom window, Dad's open bottle of Amaretto on the dresser, Bon Jovi's "Slippery When Wet" blaring on the boombox. I must admit, folks…it wasn't a pretty picture. Look…I may not have been the sharpest cheese in the fridge, but I knew how to have a good time. It was at that moment that Arlene saw Dad didn't have me under control, so she began to ramp up her discipline of me. It was a mistake she would soon regret.

My step-brother was an OK guy and we generally got along. He was really into baseball and was kind of a jock. He would have the occasional party, but they were rather mild. A keg and some pizzas on a Saturday night was their idea of a party. They weren't really sure how to handle me and my friends. Especially when one of my friends puked in his closest after wandering upstairs during one of my parties. The middle sister was a nightmare. Her and my father were constantly butting heads. She was as rebellious as I was, in female form. She would get in trouble and retaliate by throwing a massive party in the house. Dad would then retaliate by doing something like taking the door off her bedroom, and she would retaliate by staying away from home for three days in a row. It never ended with those two. But she was not intelligent enough to learn that Dad doesn't punish you for parties he doesn't see. She would always throw her parties at times when we knew Dad and Arlene would be coming home, so she would always get caught. Rookie move. The oldest sister had moved out already and we only saw her from time to time. She seemed cool, but I had very little interaction with her.

One aspect of life there that wasn't enjoyable, was my step-mother. We just never saw eye to eye. Looking back on it, it's entirely possible it could've been because I was seeing any adult woman as my mother at that point, and it's also possible it was because she was a raving bitch. Man, my father really knew how to pick 'em. Arlene and I would get into nearly constant arguments about every imaginable aspect of life once she decided to take the disciplinary reigns on me. We were just constantly butting heads like two rams on a mountainside. This put extraordinary strain and pressure on my father. On one hand, she was his wife. And on the other hand, I was his firstborn who he finally got custody of after so many years. I can't imagine it was easy on him. In many cases, Arlene would telephone my father at work after one of our arguments to tell him what happened and explain to him how miserable I was to be around. The feeling was mutual. I had always resented the fact that Arlene had a good paying job when she met my father, but after the marriage, she quit her job as Dad was back to working three jobs to keep the bills paid. So, I would often let her know about my dislike for that situation by calling her a gold digger. That would only escalate things even further.

One Saturday, during the summer after I graduated eighth grade, Arlene and I were arguing about taking out the garbage. Looking back, I could've just taken out the garbage and been on my way, but I was in full blown "stand my ground" mode, and we just continued to scream at each other. At the apex of our screaming, she yelled out that she was going to call my father, but I was next to the phone. See, in those days, you had a big ass phone with a cord that was attached to the wall in the kitchen. Well, I ripped that phone off the wall and threw it at her, hitting her in the head so bad that it sent her flying to the ground. She crawled away to the phone in her bedroom where she called my father and gave him an ultimatum…it was her or me. Dad raced home while I waited in the driveway for him. Arlene was just inside the house, in the kitchen. When Dad arrived home, he literally pulled onto the front lawn at what seemed like fifty miles an hour. As he exited the car, Arlene raced out to meet him, but he was already telling me to pack my bags. Arlene assumed this meant he was finally kicking me out. Instead, he packed his bags as well and told Arlene it was over. He just walked out on her. Obviously, I was a major factor in that move, but I have to believe there were underlying circumstances involved or else he wouldn't have pulled the trigger on such a move so quickly. After all, he had a great paying job with tons of benefits, a nice house in a quiet suburb, and life was finally back on track after my mother left him out to dry. There had to me more to it. We packed, left, and were at my grandfather's house in Linton in just a few hours. I would never see Arlene, or her kids, again. Thankfully.

Within days we had a house for ourselves. Once again, another change of scenery for me. Starting over once again. This time as a freshman in high school. As you can imagine, I once again struggled to fit in with kids that had been going to school together their entire lives. I had now gone through one set of friends in elementary school, that weren't even from the town I was living in, to another set of friends for two years at a different junior high, to a brand-new set of classmates as a freshman not only in another town, but another state. But, just as I had done before, I made new friends and persevered.

The house Dad bought was a tiny little shack on E Street in Linton. It was a two-bedroom, one-bathroom ranch with a living room and kitchen. The washer and dryer were in the kitchen and it had an unusable one-car carport. It couldn't have been more than 800 square feet, tops. I had a mattress on the floor and all my clothes in the one and only closet in the house, which was in the one bathroom we had, which adjoined both bedrooms. Dad had a bed and one dresser. He got himself a job in a machine shop in Indianapolis, two hours away. He wasn't happy with his new situation, and I couldn't blame him. The height of his frustration came while traveling to work one morning. The station wagon he had died as he came over a hill just outside of Indianapolis and he literally coasted to the bottom of the hill. There he found a car dealership. Not having time to waste, or much money to spend, he quickly made a deal to trade in the old family truckster and would drive off the lot with a new Chevy S10 pickup...complete with no air conditioning, manual transmission, only an AM radio, and manual windows. He was so aggravated he had to buy that truck out of necessity. You could just see the defeat on his face day after day. And he definitely didn't want to be back in Linton, even if it was where he was born.

But I loved Linton. I had a tight knit bunch of friends in high school. There was everyone's favorite hippie, Danial. There was Sean, the kid who used to jump off the roof of his house every day in the name of KISS. Then there was Barry and Crystal, who had an on again, off again romance for years. Leda was the one who hosted the wildest parties, hands down. And of course, there were many others like Rebecca, Tanya, Jana, Timberly, Jared, Kelly, Dale, Dennis, and Jennifer.

I was being introduced to the life of parting by my cousin, so this is where my good times really started to take on a whole new level of intensity. As a freshman, I started out as sort of a jock. I was on the football team, albeit riding the bench most of the time, and I was clean cut with a flat top. Being on the football team was an experience unto itself. Our coaches were, shall we say, devoted to their calling. Our arch rivals were the Dugger Bulldogs. Dugger was the next small town over, and our sports teams had been at war for years. Every week, during the final practice before game night, the coaches would have a spirit raising pep speech on the fifty-yard line that ended with the team tearing apart a large white sheet that the coaches had spray painted various things about the other team on. We players would then wear the scraps of that sheet we tore from it on game day in some fashion on ourselves. But the pep speech the last practice before the Dugger game was amped up a few notches. The JV coach came onto the field dressed as the grim reaper, including full face paint. He was carrying a sickle, from the end of which hung a stuffed bulldog toy. He gave a serious, low toned speech about how undeserving the Bulldogs were to even share a field with us. As the speech progressed, his tone amped up, until he had the whole team thirsty for blood. He then took the stuffed bulldog off the sickle, ripped its head off with his teeth, and exposed the fake blood he had placed inside it. Like I said…Bulldog week was insane in Miner country.

I began the year hanging out with the other football players, but all they ever did was get pass out drunk and tell tales about chasing cheerleaders. Not exactly my scene. By the end of my freshman year I was the hair metal kid who wore ripped jeans, combat boots, a rock band T-shirt and a flannel everywhere I went. My hair was long, and my left ear was pierced with a black pearl earring. From then on, I would always have a pack of smokes and a lighter on me at all times. I went from never having touched marijuana to never being without a sack of weed on me at all times. The transformation was radical, to say the least. But I was fitting in somewhere…finally. My friends and I would cruise town on Friday and Saturday nights, stopping in to parking lot after parking lot, seeing who was hanging out, and who wanted to get high. Everyone would have music blaring through the open windows of their cars and the music filled the air of the cruising strip through town like an outdoor concert. I can still see my first car…a white Pontiac Sunfire hatchback with a Batman sticker in the back window. I paid $600.00 for that baby, and I got every penny's worth in the mileage I put on cruising the strip. The jocks usually hung out in the parking lot outside the Long John Silvers on the east end of town. Stoners were broken up into groups in the parking strip in front of the town park, the "free parking" next to the gas station, and sometimes in the roller rink parking lot on the west end of town. If you wanted to drink in those days, you better buy your "Sunday beer" on Saturday night, because of Indiana's blue laws.

Immediately following the completion of my freshman year, my father informed me that he was moving back to the Chicagoland area to find better work and gave me the choice of returning with him or staying where I was. I was only fifteen at the time, so it kind of shocked me that he was even giving me the choice. See, Dad had worked since he was eight years old, so the fact that I was fifteen meant, to him, I was old enough to be on my own. Naturally I chose to stay. I finally had a group of close friends that I wasn't being forced to leave, so why would I choose to be uprooted again? So, my father gave me the keys to the house and suggested I get a job to keep my belly full. And that's exactly what I did. I started working at the local McDonald's, which literally had just opened that summer and was the only McDonald's the town ever had. To show you how old I am, I remember working for McDonald's when the news came in that they were raising the federal minimum wage to $3.15 per hour. We were excited as hell at that news. We didn't know what we were going to do with all that money. Of course, back in those days a pack of smokes cost us around $.85, and a gallon of gas was around $.78, and you could roll by Fat Pams house and pick up joints for $2.50 or get three for $5.00. So, if you had a twenty-dollar bill on you, you got a pack of smokes, three joints, and enough gas to cruise the strip all night. Get three friends together that all have twenty bucks on them, and you had yourself one helluva night.

Once we would get enough weed and gas money together, the inevitable cruise out to the country commenced. Star Lake was always my destination of choice. I remember picking up this girl one time who promised me a blow job once we got to Star Lake. I was taking those tight gavel road turns like I was Ted Kennedy and the liquor store was closing in five minutes. But my exuberance got the better of me, and I fish tailed out of control, and dropped my car in a ditch. In retrospect, turning to my companion and asking if the offer still stood was probably not the best idea. It was a long, silent walk back to town that night. Oh well, you win some…you lose some.

So now I was a working man, but with no parental supervision, a complete disdain for authority, and a penchant for the devil's lettuce. What came next was probably inevitable. I dropped out of school six weeks into my sophomore year. I was old enough to legally make that decision and there was no adult in the picture to stop me, so I just stopped going to school. About six weeks into my sophomore year I found myself sitting in my house, alone, wondering where everyone was. Duh…they were in school. Damn. Maybe I should go, too. You know…check it out and see what was happening. One day I just showed up after not being there at all since the beginning of the school year. The principal said it was time for a little chat. He explained to me that I can't just show up six weeks into the school year and pop into a class. I had some ground to make up. A lot of ground. I told him that wasn't happening, and he suggested maybe I'd be happier if I didn't come back. I agreed, and I left the building, never to return. To this day I still haven't stepped foot back inside that school. To show you how little I actually attended classes, I left school six weeks into my sophomore year with a total of 1.5 credits from my entire high school career. I just hated school with a passion.

My house became the party house. Everyone had a good time at Toms' house, and all were welcome. Life was almost perfect, but there was still that pesky job that got in the way of my good times. That changed one weird, fateful day. In the small town of Linton, there were roughly a dozen people that sold weed at that time. I've already told you about my dealer of choice, Fat Pam, but there were others as well, each one with their own select group of customers. One Saturday morning, around 2:00 am, a friend and I wandered over to Pam's place to pick up some sticky icky for our trip that day to Sunset Lake to do a little swimming. We smoked and swam all morning having the time of our lives without a care in the world. Sunset Lake was a cool place to blaze up and go swimming because it was a lake they taught scuba diving at. Because of that, there were several items sunk in the lake including a few cars, an airplane, and a school bus. The bus was near the shallow end where you dove in. It rested on an underwater ledge in such a manner that the tail end of the bus was only about five feet under the water, and the nose of the bus was straight down from there. We would swim down and enter the rear of the bus and see if we could swim all the way down to the driver's seat before needing to turn around for air. We were idiots. Since this was well before pagers and cell phones and anything resembling social media, we didn't receive the news that the cops had raided every weed dealer in town at the same time, including Fat Pam. This presented quite the predicament as the entire town went dry overnight. As you can imagine, this sent a panic through the whole town. There was no weed to be found anywhere. Then, a much older, but very good friend of mine we called Mater, approached me about a business proposition. It turns out that all but two of the dealers that got arrested in the raid were supplied with their product from one man in town. And because he wasn't selling to the masses like everyone else, he was still standing when the dust settled, but he had nobody to help distribute his products. So, he called together a few people to change that. Mater was brought in to begin selling weed to the local bar scene. Another man nicknamed Eight Ball was brought in to sell cocaine to the bikers. And I was brought in to sell weed to the high school aged kids, since that was my crowd. So, I began dealing weed and left McDonald's. The hours were far better than the Golden Arches and the money was off the chain. I had so much that I never walked the streets with empty pockets. Now I was really making a name for myself. What I didn't know was that other people were paying attention to that name.

When returning home one night, I pulled up to my house to notice my father's truck in the driveway…along with a local police cruiser and a county cop cruiser. This was surely not a good sign, especially since Dad was living four hours away. When I entered the house, I found my father and the two officers sitting in the living room. To say my father looked pissed would be an understatement. He was furious. On the coffee table were pictures of me selling weed to people at the local park. They had been watching to see who would pick up the weed distribution mantle in town, and they found me. They sat in the farthest part of the park, in the dark, and took pictures of me dealing out of my car. There was no denying it at this point…they had me. I was busted. But my family was prominent in the town and they were willing to give me a break for my family's sake. I wouldn't be arrested if I left town and didn't come back. In the immediacy of the moment, that deal sounded damn good to me, so I packed my stuff and went back to Chicago that night. I would stay with my father and step-mother, Josephine, for a short period of time before venturing out on my own again. Dad and Jo had gotten married a few years before, and, once again, I was the best man. It was a small ceremony held in the living room of Jo's cousin, Anette. You have to hand it to the old man, he may have lacked a lot of things in life, but he sure wasn't lacking in the balls department. It takes a lot of balls to stand at the alter a third time, when the first two marriages wiped you out.

They were living in the house Jo was left by her parents in Berwyn, Illinois. It was a classic Chicago style bungalow on 26ᵗʰ street. The house just looked like a piece of Chicago history. A true classic. I had the opportunity to come up and visit with them a couple times while I was still living in Linton. One visit was noteworthy indeed. My friend, Danial, and I came up for a weekend to see the sights and relax. We only brought a couple joints with us, but I had smoked with Jo-Jo once before, so I knew she could get some weed if we really needed it. Sure enough, we smoked all of our weed in very short order, and soon I found myself asking Jo to score for us. While she was cool with smoking and would partake in a little of the devil's lettuce herself, she didn't feel comfortable hooking us up because my father was still stuck in his antiquated ways when it came to the subject of the sticky icky, so she declined. But she did make us a deal…if we could find the quarter ounce of weed she had hidden in the house, she would give us as much as we wanted. Seriously? Oh…it's game on now! Danial and I must have searched every nook and cranny of that bungalow looking for her stash. We searched every closet, every drawer, every old coffee can full of nails in the garage…everywhere. We found nothing. In three days of searching we managed to find nothing. On the morning we were set to leave, Jo came into the bedroom Danial and I were staying in and sat down next to me on the bed I was using that weekend. She asked if I had found her weed, to which I told her that we had, in fact, failed at that endeavor. She then stood up, lifted the mattress to the bed, and pulled out the much sought-after sack of goodness. I had been sleeping on it the entire time It was the one place we had never thought to look in. She fooled us. While we didn't get any weed out of that deal, I did learn a lesson…ALWAYS check under the mattress for the sweet, sticky bud.

Living with Dad and Jo was OK. I once again was given a bedroom in the basement. It seems as if I was destined to dwell underground. They let me come and go as I pleased, but I was limited as I didn't have a car at the time. I worked and kept a little money in my pocket, but you could tell that Dad and Jo didn't really want me around. They had raised their kids and were done, and here I was coming back to live with them. Dad was particularly upset given the way I was forced to leave Linton. I wasn't exactly thrilled with my situation either. Here I was, having been living on my own and partying every day, now living in my Dad's basement, with my second step-mother, and working at McDonald's. This was simply not a life I even remotely wanted, so I sought to change it any way I could.

Dad offered me a position at the machine shop he was working at. He was the night manager, and I had grown up around micrometers and calipers my whole life, so I gave it a shot. Dad saw this as a chance to finally get me into the industry he had worked in his whole life. I saw it as a way to make better money than fast food, but not for long. I operated machines under Dad's watchful eye, and always found myself staring out the window. I hated working indoors. And working under Dad made it all the more stressful. it wasn't long before I would decide to break out on my own once more. Only this time I wasn't going to be chained down. This time I was hitting the road. This time I was going to keep the wind at my back and my feet on the ground

Tom Powell Jr.

"IF IN DOUBT, JUST WALK UNTIL YOUR DAY
BECOMES INTERESTING." – ROLF POTTS

CHAPTER SEVEN
My thumb in the air and the wind in my hair

After living with my father and Jo-Jo for a short period of time, I hooked up with a carnival. Yeah, you read that right...I was a carny. When I worked at the McDonald's in Cermak Plaza in Berwyn, I met a guy who had worked for a carnival from time to time. He would go on and on about how cool working for the carnival was, and I became intrigued. One day he called to tell me that the carnival he had worked for was coming back through town, and that they were paying fifty dollars cash to any able-bodied person willing to help with the setup of the rides. Well, at that point in my life, fifty bucks was a huge deal, so naturally I agreed to work on helping the set-up crew. He and I went to the site, where I was introduced to the owner of the carnival. He was an older man, with a slight humpback. He lived out of a fifth wheel camper with his wife and two small dogs. I don't think he thought I was anything special. Nothing more than another body to help move the heavy pieces of the rides in order to facilitate a faster set up. I did my day's work, and it was a tough day's work, and got my pay. To me, that was where it started and ended...just another day's work, and a quick fifty bucks. At the end of the week, I was asked if I wanted to help with the tear down of the carnival for another fifty dollars, and of course, I accepted. I guess I did a good job, because the owner asked me if I wanted to meet them in the next town to assist with the setup and teardown once again. Again, I accepted because fifty bucks was still fifty bucks. When I arrived to work my setup day, some of the rides were already set up, and I was called over to speak to the head maintenance man in charge of the carnival. He explained to me that one of the tires that helps to rotate the ride called The Zipper was flat and needed to be changed. This required someone to climb up to the tire, which was about forty feet in the air, and take the flat tire off, then carry that flat tire back down, before heading back up with a new tire to install it. I really didn't think much about it and I set out to change that tire. Upon completing the task I was given, I was once again called over to speak to the head maintenance man, only this time he was with the owner of the carnival. They told me that they liked the way I worked and wanted to offer the job of running the Zipper full time. Given that I was a free spirit, and wanted to do a bit of traveling, I jumped at the opportunity. This was exactly what I was looking for in my life. I wanted to get out of Dad and Jo's place, I hated working fast food and at the machine shop, so I went all-in and hit the road. What the hell did I have to lose? The pay was forty-five dollars a day, cash, during the days the carnival was open to the public, and one hundred dollars a day on setup and teardown days. At the time, it was a sweet deal, especially considering I would have no bills other than food while traveling from town to town. So, I purged down my personal possessions and made sure everything I owned would fit into a hiking backpack, and I hit the road to work as a carney.

Most people have a very specific view of what a carny is, and for the most part, those views are correct, but I wasn't your typical carny. I showered every day after work, I was interested in world affairs, and I didn't spend every waking hour trying to figure out how to get my hands on more drugs. Still, I fit in with the carnival family very well. Perhaps it was the free-spirited nature one has to possess to work in such a field…a love of not being tied down to anything. After all, if one has nothing, then one has nothing that will hurt them.

Traveling with the carnival was a very interesting, and unique, way of life. The boss had a few drivers that would move the rides from one town to the next every Monday. When they would pull the rides into town, they would spot them exactly where they needed to be set on the site. All of us workers would figure out how to get the next town by whatever means we could. A couple guys had cars, and some rode with the truck drivers…if the truck drivers were in the mood to have a tag along. Others of us chose to hitchhike. That was my preferred way of travel. There's something very freeing about having everything you own on your back, putting your thumb in the air, and just seeing what the day will bring your way. At that time, people were far more willing to pick up a hitchhiker than they are today, so catching a ride was never difficult.

Tuesday was set up day. Everyone worked all day, and into the night, setting up the rides, pulling electric cables, making sure the ticket booths were in place, and putting any finishing touches on that were needed. Wednesday through Sunday we were open for business. You would do a full ride inspection every day before opening, and then you'd open. Open days were the best. Each of the major ride attractions would be given a stereo system to crank the tunes on, and thus help draw in the crowds.

After a brief time operating The Zipper, I was given a ride called the Force Ten. It was a puke inducing ride for sure. But because it was the new ride the boss just bought, I was given a killer sound system, and an assistant. The boss anticipated heavy ridership since it was the shiny new attraction, and he was right. I was packed every night. And because the ride was always jammed with people, the crowds around my ride were always huge. This made it easier to sneak girls on to the ride for free through one of the exit gates. Once I hit the button to initiate the ride sequence, I had ninety seconds until the ride finished its run. I would use that time to scope out girls near the front of the line. Then, like I was some kind of road manager for a rock group, I would randomly pull girls out of line and direct them to the exit and tell them to wait there until the ride was finished. Once everyone exited, the girls were allowed on first, and then the gate opened for paying customers. This was before my gray hair and before my gut grew. I had a chin. I was in shape. It was easy to get girls to do what I wanted back then. I had very long hair, but the sides of my head were shaved, so when my hair was down, it looked like just another full head of glorious '80s metal hair. But when I pulled it back into a ponytail, I exposed the Mohawk nature of the hair-do, and it just completed the picture. Just your above average, incredibly sexy, heavily tattooed carny rolling through your town, chasing after your daughter with a pocket full of weed and a wild streak the size of Texas.

It goes without saying that at this stage in my life, I would get stares and mumbled background conversation everywhere I went. "Is that a man or a woman?" "Can you believe the filth the carnival brings into town?" "I bet he's on drugs!" Yeah…I've heard all of that from restaurants to parks to the local 7-11. One time, while playing a spot on the west side of Chicago, a fellow carny and I were stopped by the local police officers and questioned. But the questioning took place in an alley. They weren't interested in doing the paperwork a couple of no-good carnies would cause them, so we got roughed up in an alley, our weed was taken, and we were left there to bleed. This wouldn't be the last time I would have the exact same experience with a member of the law enforcement community before my time on the road was over.

After we closed every night, the entire crew consolidated into one big cleanup crew and we would all clean every inch of the site before being paid and relieved of duty for the night. After close of business on Sunday night, everyone in the crew, along with some locals hired for the night, would tear the rides down once again and prep them for their Monday journey to the next town. That's it. That was the schedule. A couple of guys had tents, and some of the guys who had a car slept in their car. But I was one of the people that either set up a tent or slept under one of the rides. There's a ride called the "Flying Bobs.", and in one section along the ride's standing platform, the

75

panels under the cars stood over seven feet off the ground. This made it possible for an average six-foot man to stand up without issue underneath the platforms. We would hang a garden hose in the under-side frame work of the panels and that was our shower. You haven't lived until you've taken an ice-cold carny shower on a crisp midwestern morning.

Our diet was 100% carnival food and fast food. There were no home cooked meals. No pot roast, no meatloaf, and no home-made pasta sauce. Just a steady diet of Taco Bell and funnel cakes. It didn't matter back then because we were young and getting our workouts in the form of man handling steel carnival ride components. Tacos became my go to food choice. We used to hit every little taco joint in whatever town we were in, and they were always great. Especially those at El Faro in Summit, Illinois. I cannot begin to tell you how many hours of my life have been spent in El Faro enjoying some spicy carrots and a taco or burrito. Dammit…now I want tacos!

After two years on the road with the carnival, an opportunity to change things up presented itself. While I was with the carnival, I had run into an old friend from my Jr High days, Adam. He introduced me to a new friend of his he met while working together named Jimmy. Jimmy and I hit it off right away. At the time, we had the exact same outlook on life. Jimmy's house was the party house and Jimmy didn't give a damn about authority. Not. One. Bit. Jimmy, I would come to learn, was a Dead Head. I had already been turned on to The Dead by their video for "Touch of Grey," and I liked it, but what I didn't know about was the entire sub-culture that accompanied The Dead. That's the world Jimmy introduced me to. He showed me that I could give up the back-breaking work of setting up and tearing down carnival rides, but still be able to travel. All I had to do was blend in to the Grateful Dead scene. So, I gave up the carnival life and hit the road following The Dead.

Life following The Dead was vastly different. No schedule, but no steady money either, which causes one's survival mode to kick in. You get creative and begin to think outside the box. We would earn money however we could, depending on the circumstances presented. In one town we would buy loaves of bread and jars of peanut butter and jelly and we would sell PB&Js to the stoned legions of locals taking in the ambiance of a Grateful Dead show parking lot. In the next town we would buy red solo cups and a variety of fruit and sell one-dollar fruit cups. Once we found a box next a dumpster with over one hundred "Have A Nice Day" bumper stickers. We sold them for a buck a piece. And every now and again you'd stumble into a deal to buy a couple of sheets of LSD and make more money in one night than we did in a month. On tour, you rapidly learn how to improvise, overcome, and adapt.

We usually kept ourselves clean in whatever local body of water we had access to, but if none was available, we would hit the closest truck stop or rest station. The truck stop showers were the worst. You felt like you needed a shower after having just taken a shower. And you'd better watch your step in a truck stop parking lot. I've seen more things go down in one of those lots than anywhere else I've ever been to. Ponds, lakes, and rivers were always the bathing destination of choice for me, if one was nearby. There are some amazing hot springs in the Ocala National Forest around the Orlando area that you just never want to get out of, if you ever find yourself camping in that part of the world.

Sleeping was always in a tent. I had a little tent that collapsed down enough to be fastened on to the outside of my hiking backpack, which would spring into shape once you threw it into the air. It was the perfect little two-person tent for life on the road. While between shows, we would frequently look for lighted billboards along the highways to camp under as it provided us with good lighting under which we could sit up and shoot the breeze. I was fond of Motel 6 billboards, because it reminded me of the old commercial, "We'll leave the light on for ya!" A little sleeping bag and a rolled-up coat made for a very comfortable bed on the road. Life was just much simpler then. To quote Metallica, wherever I laid my head was home.

And the communal spirit of the Heads was amazing. You really were part of a family on tour. I'm here to tell you that the hippie spirit did not die in the sixties. The Heads kept it alive long after the calendar changed from the sixties to the seventies. You will never again experience anything like the parking lots in those days. It was literally an entire nomadic town of hippies that just moved their tents and busses from one town to the next, selling their goods and living as freely as possible. These people had no bank accounts or forwarding addresses. They weren't filing taxes or appearing for jury duty. These people didn't exist. They were ghosts, blowing in and out of your town so quickly you barely felt their effect. And they all looked out for one another. Some of the best people I've ever known were people I knew living on tour. This was truly an amazing period in my life. There were no bills. Nothing was due. I didn't owe anyone anything, and nobody was looking for me.

This was when nature changed from a small patch of green in an urban setting to becoming an integral part of my everyday life. This was nature in all its glory. Nobody was racing to get out of the rain. Quite the opposite, in fact. When it rained, we made sure we were out in it, soaking up all of that live giving nourishment the sky was returning to the earth. Our skin was constantly tanned from being in the sun all day. We felt every bit of nature with every mile we walked, and state we crossed. It was freedom in its purest form.

My attire went from ripped jeans, rock tees, and work boots to shorts, sandals, and a tie dye, 24 hours a day. I had one hoodie to keep me warm on the occasional chilly night, and a steal your face denim baseball cap completed the ensemble. And a Dead Lot always provided a large array of foods to choose from. The tacos…oh sweet jesus, the tacos. Many a morning I would roll out of the tent, stagger over to one of the food tents, and start my day off with a few nice steak tacos. Seriously…can you think of anything better? Free as a jaybird, livin' on the road, and starting your day of with steak tacos. Perfection.

The shows The Dead put on were spectacles unto themselves. The atmosphere of a Dead show is something that simply cannot be duplicated. Every show was a vast sea of tie dyed shirts, a constant haze of smoke emanating from the copious amounts of dank being consumed, and a vibrant spirit that can only be felt inside a Dead concert. The music seemed to flow through each venue as if it was dancing on the smoke that twisted and turned in the night air. No matter what city, or what time of day, Jerry and the boys always seemed to be on top of their game. The crowd knew every song from its first note but were always treated to incredible improvisational jams that differed each night. If you weren't dancing at a Dead show, you weren't breathing. There was no way to avoid it while having your chest cavity rocked by the steady beat of dual drummers and the symphonic flow of the keyboard. And when Jerry and Bob were on their games, which was often, it was pure bliss. From the smooth steady sounds of "China Cat Sunflower," to the upbeat tempo of "Mexicali Blues," to the crowd rockin "U.S. Blues," we were treated to the sounds that linked every one of us with each new show. A tab of acid and a solid song set could transport you to another world. To every Dead Head from that era, always remember this…. the earth is over four billion years old, and somehow, we were lucky enough to be alive at the same time as the Grateful Dead. We were lucky.

During my time following The Dead, I got the chance to travel to Indiana, D.C., Oregon, California, Ohio, Pennsylvania, New York, Massachusetts, Phoenix, Georgia, Florida, Seattle, Las Vegas, Vermont, St. Louis, Michigan, New

Jersey, Maryland, Colorado, Utah, North Carolina, Tennessee, Alabama, and all points in between. All on foot or hitch hiking, and all while living in a tent with everything I owned in a backpack. If I had a Fitbit back then, it would have blown up.

After some more time on the road, we once again found ourselves back in Chicago for another Dead show, only this time it was summer time. July in Chicago can be beautiful when rolling into town on the Dead Tour. The familiarity of rolling into the downtown area on a bright, sunny day, watching the boats on Lake Michigan and seeing the fountain again just made you realize you were "home." The band, as always, played a stellar last show in Chicago before heading into a small break from touring. Just a couple months to rest the weary old bones. This gave us a chance to crash at Jimmy's mother's house in Cicero and find some temporary work to replenish the traveling reserves for the next leg of the tour. Jimmy had worked on the grounds crew at Brookfield Zoo, and got to know some people in the landscape industry, so he was able to get us jobs at a mulch and firewood yard chopping, and stacking, firewood. Jimmy's brother was with us and took a job at the mulch yard as well. To this day I can't remember why I wasn't working on August 9th, 1995, but I will never forget what happened that day that changed my life forever. Jerry Garcia died. I saw it on the news at Jimmy's house while he and his brother were at work. I remember just staring at the TV trying to figure out if what I had just heard was true. I mean, it couldn't be true. We just saw him play a month ago. Jerry Garcia doesn't die. What cruel, twisted prank was this? But it wasn't a prank. It was real. This actually happened. Jerry was gone. I knew I had to tell Jimmy, but this was before cell phones and Facebook and Twitter and even pagers. And since there was no phone in the mulch yard, the only way I had of informing them was to drive out to work and tell them. The news hit them like a ton of bricks. Rich, Jimmy's brother, just fell to his knees in stunned silence. It couldn't be real.

That night, Dead Heads by the thousands gathered atop a little hill along the Lake Michigan coast called Cricket Hill located in Montrose Harbor. I've never seen so many Dead Heads be so silent. It was surreal. As the crowd shared joint after joint with each other, the discussion of the day's news was all that was on anyone's lips. The patriarchal leader of the movement was gone, and with it went our entire way of life. No more touring. No next city. No next Dead lot. Nothing. It was all over. We were shacked up in Jimmy's mother house in Cicero, with zero path forward. Decisions had to be made.

One decision that should've never been made was the night Jimmy and I decided to become international criminals. Look.... we were drunk as hell, tripping on two hits of acid each, and had completely lost all sense of reality that night. I had gotten myself a little second floor apartment in Berwyn, where Jimmy would frequently crash. Jimmy and I were in the midst of re-painting the living room walls when we decided to start tripping. That's usually when things go off the rails. During our psychedelic, alcohol infused painting session, we began to talk about life without the Dead, and what we were going to do with ourselves. The idea of getting real jobs and not traveling anymore really sucked to us. As the conversation progressed, and the effects of the LSD grew in intensity, we made a life decision. We were going to head to Mexico and hook up with a drug cartel and begin our journey to becoming international criminals like Pablo Escobar. I know...best idea ever, right? Wait...it gets better. The sheer idiocy with which we laid out specific details of this plan are stunning in their magnitude. We knew we would have to steal our way south, since we didn't have the funds to make it to Mexico, but we had no real means by which to rob anyone. Jimmy had an old, non-working revolver of his father's, but that was it. We had no ammunition, but it didn't matter, because the gun wasn't functional anyway. But it was intimidating enough to see, so we thought we could use sheer intimidation for the first leg of our trip. The plan was to travel to northwest Indiana, where we would use the non-working gun to rob some random gas station to get enough funds to make it south to the area of Indiana I have ties to. Once there, we would rob a bait and tackle shop I knew of that had tons of hunting supplies, including guns and archery supplies. Now I may have begun to lose some of you here thinking this isn't believable, but it's all 100% true. We planned to take all the provisions and weapons we needed to get us to Mexico. To show you how stunningly high and idiotically stupid we were, we ordered a pizza and rehashed the plan to make sure we had all the details laid out.

Once we decided that our plan had been perfected down to the last detail, I packed a bag, and we split for Jimmy's house. I literally left the door to the apartment open, radio on, and the paint still in the open can on the living room floor. Who cares? I'm never coming back. By the time we got to Jimmy's, he packed a bag, and we were back on the road, it was around midnight. I needed to top off the tank before we could even make it to northwest Indiana, so I stopped at what at the time was an Amoco station at Harlem Avenue and Pershing, in Stickney, Illinois. Jimmy needed to use the bathroom, but they refused him access at that time of night. He asked me to try and get the key because he thought they were spooked by his appearance. I was just as unsuccessful as he was at gaining entry. The fact that I had on ripped jeans, black leather studded cowboy boots, a T-shirt with a yellow smiley face that had a bullet hole in the head, and hair down to my shoulders probably didn't help matters. Not to worry...we're no strangers to a middle of the night outdoors leak. I pulled around the corner and stopped on a side street. Jimmy hopped out to take care of business, and I seized the opportunity to revisit the map one more time. Once Jimmy got back into the car, we once again prepared to embark on our journey. I looked to my left, and again to my right, and saw everything was clear, so I looked down, put my foot on the brake, turned the car on and looked up. That's when I saw the ten squad cars surrounding us, and the cop tapping on my window with his flashlight. Either those guys materialized via a hole in the space time continuum, or I was so high that what seemed like seconds was actually minutes.

The next thing I know is Jimmy and I are being yanked out of the car by what seemed to be an army of rather irritated police officers. When Jimmy exited the car to relieve himself, what he didn't know he was doing was relieving himself on the lawn of a Stickney police officer, who called the boys in blue to have a little chat with us. Awesome. When Jimmy returned to the vehicle, he cracked open a cold one for the ride and had it sitting between his legs. As he was pulled from the car, that beer spilled on the officer's shoes. I can still hear the officer's voice as he smugly said "Ya got a little spillage there, eh buddy?" We were in the shit now. Before I could ascertain what was happening, there were two cops in my car, going over every inch of it. Naturally, they found Jimmy's revolver under the passenger seat, and the next words I heard were "Whose gun?" followed immediately by Jimmy saying, "What gun?" BOOM...now we found ourselves slammed against the trunk of the car and getting to know our local law enforcement officers in a real personal way. Eventually there was beer, a little weed, two fully packed bags, and a revolver sitting on the roof of my car, Jimmy and I were in handcuffs, and we were getting personally escorted to the nearest jail cell. We're talkin top notch service all the way. I had to enjoy my stay in the pokey sans footwear since the officer deemed the large studs on my boots to be dangerous, saying I could roundhouse someone and knock them unconscious with them. Excuse me? Have you seen the condition I'm in? I have at least seven miller genuine drafts in me and I'm trippin' balls. I couldn't roundhouse anything even if my life depended on it. Nonetheless, they took my damn boots. Immediately I began pacing my cell, thinking about how we were going to get out of this. Meanwhile, Jimmy was passed out cold in his cell. He figured he might as well get some sleep since we were already caught.

81

When we were booked, the cops were basically just using us for late night entertainment. They knew we were wasted on something, and they couldn't stop laughing. Jimmy kept tapping away at a typewriter sitting on the desk next to him, and the cops were just watching him and laughing. I was twitching like a jackrabbit on cocaine. It seemed as if they knew we shouldn't be out driving, but that we were probably harmless. Neither of us ever came clean about what we were doing. Eventually it came time to bail out. Neither of us called anyone, because we had enough on us to bail one of us out. The plan was to bail Jimmy out, have him walk back to his house, and get the remaining bail to come get me out, so Jimmy was set free, and I began to wait. Jimmy's house was about a ten-minute walk from the police station, so when we hit the two-hour mark, and he still hadn't returned, the cops took mercy on me and released me on an I-bond. I walked to Jimmy's house to find out what happened to him, only to find him passed out in his bed. Typical Jimmy. I woke him up and we started hoofing it towards his girlfriend's house to see if we could scrape up some money. She gave us the money to get my car out of the impound, but was so pissed, she wouldn't let Jimmy hold his son, and slammed the door in his face as we left. We now faced an hour walk to the impound yard to retrieve the car. As soon as we got back into the car, Jimmy grabbed the map and started talking about northwest Indiana again. I told him he was nuts. Dude…we have an impending court case now. We can't go anywhere. Yeah, a night in jail makes you go from international criminal to law abiding citizen really quick.

We eventually got ahold of my father, who promptly chewed me a new ass for not calling while I was in jail. What did he expect? The man had been telling me my entire life not to call him if I ever got arrested, and when I actually listen to him, he's pissed. I can't win. Dad arranged for us to meet a lawyer that was a friend of the family. Talk about shady. This guy met Jimmy and I to discuss the case in a closed bar in Bellwood. But, he was helping us out, so I didn't look a gift horse in the mouth. Eventually the case was heard, and we were both convicted of "unlawful use of a weapon" and "unlawful possession of a handgun." Nothing a future expungement couldn't handle, but a bit of a wake-up call none the less. Those cops most likely prevented us from doing some really stupid shit that could've ruined our lives forever. I dodged a major bullet with that one.

The four years I spent on the road between the carnival and following The Dead were some of the best years of my life. I was afforded the opportunity to live as freely as I ever have, and I was able to see much of this great country, up close and personal. Some of the nicest people I've ever met were met while I was on the road. There is something about not having to worry about the trappings of society that enables people to just be themselves. There are no Jones' to keep up with. There is just an absolute enjoyment of life. A chance to see the real you. The you that isn't layered under the latest trends or the most popular fad. There was just my thumb in the air and the wind in my hair, and I loved every damn second of it.

"ENJOYMENT OF THE LANDSCAPE IS A
THRILL." ~ DAVID HOCKNEY

CHAPTER EIGHT
People pay you to mow their lawn?

As I mentioned earlier in this book, Jimmy had connections in the landscape world through his time at Brookfield Zoo, so he lined himself up a job as a lawn mowing laborer with a one-man operation out of Berwyn, after that initial brief stint at the mulch yard. The guy needed another laborer, so I was asked if I wanted the job. I literally had never heard of anyone paying someone else to mow their lawn before this. My family, and all the families around us, always mowed their own lawns, so this was a totally foreign concept to me. But, I needed some steady income, and there weren't many options presenting themselves, so I went to work mowing lawns the rest of that summer. I went back to breaking my back again, but at least I was still outside, and I didn't really mind the work. It was unique. I was starting to enjoy it. We were mowing postage stamp sized lots in the Berwyn and Cicero area with 21" push mowers a few days a week and doing light landscape construction work the remainder of the week. It wasn't bad, but it wasn't exciting either. And now that I was in the industry, I was beginning to notice other landscape crews, and I was noticing what they were doing. My intrigue level spiked once again.

That winter we got laid off, as tends to happen in the landscape industry in the winter, so we hit the road for the gulf coast once again. This time it was much easier with the money we earned from landscaping. We would usually spend our time off floating around the gulf coast area from Tampa, all the way around to the east end of Texas. New Orleans was always a must-stop destination for our winter travels. If you haven't had a chance to attend a Mardi Gras, please do so. You will never experience anything like it anywhere. Trust me. I have had the privilege to attend three Mardi Gras and it is the ultimate party. Wow. As I said, these winter road trips were easier with the landscape money we had, and the system was really working. We could work all summer and travel all winter. It was the best of both worlds. Jimmy would stay at his mother's house for the summer and I would always get a little apartment somewhere cheap. I would furnish the place with used furnishings I came across, or Good Will furniture. At the end of each landscape season, I would sell everything in the apartment, notify the landlord I was splitting, and hit the road again.

The second winter I worked in landscaping, we initially headed to North Carolina to spend a little time with a friend of Jimmy's brother. He was living in Blowing Rock, North Carolina, which is very close to the college town of Boone. When we first rolled into Boone, we decided to park the car for bit to conserve on gas, and just take in the campus on foot. It seemed like a hoppin' place and we were looking to party. As we walked down one street, we noticed a small gathering of folks outside a garden apartment door, and one person had an acoustic guitar with them. From a distance, it looked like it might be our kind of people. You could clearly see through the opened door that the apartment was packed with people. We had to check this out. As we approached the gathering outside of the apartment, we asked what was going on. We were met with very big smiles and a very warmly delivered "Come on in! We're having a praise party!" They were holy rollers. Not a drop of alcohol or a spec of sticky icky to be found. It was going to be a hard pass from us.

That night, as we continued to meet more and more locals, we heard the stories of a man named Bear who was the local drug source. We were told he lived in a place called "Camelot," and when we found Camelot, we'd find what we were looking for. Finally, someone told us where we could find Camelot. It was a small group of town homes nestled up on the side of a mountain. We got in the car and headed in that direction. As we climbed the road leading to the community, we noticed the dozens and dozens of cars parked along the side of the road, and knew we had to be close. We found a spot to park and continued the climb on foot. Upon reaching Camelot, what we discovered was two, four-unit townhouse buildings, with only one unit being occupied…Bear's. The place was packed with people that spilled out into the front of the dwelling. We made our way inside the split level and went up to the second floor where there was a living room, dining room, kitchen and bathroom. Not one spec of furniture could be found. Just wall to wall people, gallons of alcohol, and all the weed you could smoke. We had found what we were looking for. We blended in with the crowd and began to party the night away. Our thick Chicago accents quickly drew the interest of many in the crowd and we became the people to meet. We were wrecked. Every joint being passed around, we took a hit. Every beer that was offered, we accepted. Every shot that was poured for us, we happily consumed. We were getting destroyed. But people were digging the "Chicago guys." We were becoming cult heroes. We began to ask about Bear because we wanted to

86

obtain some "personal vegetables" for our stay in the Tar Heel State. We were directed to the lower level, where there was a bathroom and three bedrooms. The last bedroom on the left was where Bear was holding court. He was in there with two of his guys and three women, smoking some dank and making sure the party goers upstairs were supplied with all the goodies needed to enjoy their night. We were brought in by someone outside the door and introduced. As it turned out, Bear had already heard stories about the two "Chicago Guys" before we even made our way downstairs, and he wanted to meet us. As with the crowd upstairs, they were fascinated with the fact that we were from Chicago and that we were just traveling by the seat of our pants. As we sat there, hotboxing the hell out of that bedroom, Bear reached into a small travel trunk he had and pulled out a sheet of acid. We were asked if wanted a tab, on the house. By this time, we were so wrecked that dropping a tab was just going to ensure this lasted well into tomorrow. Naturally, we accepted the tabs offered. Now we were tripping our asses off, in a stranger's house, our first night in North Carolina. Life is good.

We would eventually find the man we were looking for and spent a great couple of days at his place. He was a vegetarian, so we ate a vegan meal while at his place. It was interesting, but not something I would ever do long term. His apartment had the best balcony that overlooked a wooded ravine along the side of a mountain. The tree canopy came right to the edge of the balcony. It was amazing. During our stay we frequently traveled to the top of the mountains to see the various peaks popping through the clouds. It was stunning. As we exited town, we stopped back in to Bear's place the morning we left. The place still looked like it had just had a party thrown in it. We were met with a loud "CHICAGO!" as we entered. We picked up some of the chronic for our trip South, and off we went. Next stop, Florida.

I don't remember much of the journey between North Carolina and Florida, but I remember waking up in Daytona beach one morning wondering where the hell we were. Some local law enforcement officers were interested in why we were sleeping on the beach as well, and we were soon chased away. We headed into Orlando, where I blew a red light, and was given a ticket. Florida wasn't being kind to us on this trip. Maybe it was time we got the hell out of the state and concentrated our efforts on the Louisiana area. So, we began to head east into the panhandle.

A couple of miles outside of Tallahassee the transmission on my car dropped. We coasted to the side of the road and stared at the car that failed to get us out of Florida. Looks like we were walking from here on. Luckily, a tow truck came by just at that moment. He told us he could tow us in to the mechanic and said it was on the house because he was heading that way anyway, and because he saw my Grateful Dead hat, so he knew we were cool. We thanked him with a little sampling of the kind bud and began discussing what needed to be done to get the car back on the road. The trans was covered under a warranty I had, but it was going to take a couple weeks to get it done. Fuck me…we're stuck here for a couple weeks. Jesus. This wasn't going to be good.

The first night, we hit a movie theatre to just relax and take our minds off things. The theatre was amazing. The seats were larger reclining type seats with tables and full menus. We ate tacos and had a few beers. I could live in that theatre. I mean, beer and tacos in a movie theatre? My god…I'm in heaven. After the movie, we snuck onto the dealership lot where my car was and slept inside my car. We were awoken the next morning by an irritated garage manager who informed us we couldn't be sleeping in the car on the lot at night. Well where the hell else are we going to sleep? We can't pitch a tent in downtown Tallahassee. We walked around that day seeing what the town had to offer and contemplating our options. As day turned into night, we began to round the edges with some Mary Jane and that brought on the munchies. It was a ravenous munchies attack. I needed something, STAT. As it was the only place open, we hit the Taco Bell. The lobby was closed, but the late-night drive through was open, so we walked up to the drive through menu and ordered. We then walked around to the window and were refused service because we weren't in a car. What? Are you kidding? Dude….my car is broken, you're the only place open, you only have the drive through open, I'm so high I can smell colors, and I have money in my hand. Quit playing games and put the tacos in the bag. Let's go. But he didn't put the tacos in the bag. Instead, he called the cops, without us knowing, and Tallahassee's finest arrived to have a little chat with us. This was now the third city we'd been to in Florida during this trip, and it was the third time we were having interactions with local law enforcement. It was time to leave the car where it was and get the hell out of Florida. I'll come back for the car when it's ready.

And away we went…eastward bound once again, only on foot this time. The goal was to stick to the original plan of getting back to New Orleans, and just lay low there for a while, then take a bus back to Florida to grab the car. That plan would've worked if not for the cops that chased us out of our tents at the rest stop in the middle of the night. This was getting ridiculous. We decided to cut our losses and just head back to Chicago for a while. So, we made our way to 75 north, and begin hitchhiking north. Just a few miles on 75 North

88

and we were picked up by four guys in a van heading to Ohio. When we asked why they stopped for us, they informed us it was because they saw I was wearing a Steal Your Face hat, so they knew we had to be cool, and that we probably had weed. They were correct on both counts. And, once again, the legend of The Dead assisted us. We rode with them all the way to Ohio, fully understanding who we were riding with when we stopped at a Waffle House in Georgia and witnessed the driver attempt to pick up a woman in the parking lot by laying the ever so smooth line of "Hey baby…you wanna drink some beer and have some sex?" on her. I'm still shocked it wasn't a more effective line.

When they dropped us off in Ohio, we were ill-prepared for the environment. See, it was February and we had been knocking around the gulf coast so long, all we had were shorts, T-shirts, and sandals. The men in the van took pity on us and gave us a couple of old blankets. We were absolutely freezing. So, we threw the blankets around us and started walking west toward Chicago in the dead of night. We didn't make it very far before an Ohio state trooper stopped to inform us we couldn't be walking along the highway. That setback sent us to the county roads, where we were even more isolated from any chance of being picked up while attempting to hitchhike. Then, as expected, we were visited by a county cop who explained to us that we couldn't just be walking down the county roads either. After explaining to him our situation, and that all we were trying to do was get back to Chicago, he drove us to an all-night diner, where three other county cops met us. After a brief discussion amongst themselves, they informed us that they would get us to the Ohio/Indiana state line, where we would once again be on our own. So, we were shuttled from one county line to the next, where we would switch squad cars for the journey to the next county line, until we finally reached Indiana. When we were dropped off at the state line, we were politely told not to come back. Somehow, I didn't think that was going to be a problem for us, and once again we put shoe sole to pavement in our continued trek westward. By this time the sun was rising, and we became even more visible to the authorities. What happened next was nothing if not predictable. We were stopped by an Indiana state trooper who wasn't quite as accommodating as the Ohio county boys were. They didn't arrest us, but they wouldn't let us continue our journey either. So, they allowed us to make a call, and I called my Aunt Rita, who came and got us as quickly as she could. She ferried us back to Jimmy's house in Cicero, and we were finally able to relax from a journey that tested our limits. We must have slept for two days. Once my car was repaired, I took a Greyhound bus from Chicago to

Tallahassee, picked up the car, and immediately drove straight back to Chicago. No stopping for me this time. This time I just wanted to get home.

After getting back home to Illinois just before the next landscape season was set to ramp up, I hooked up with a different landscape company as a laborer on a construction crew. Initially I thought I had made a massive mistake. This work was even more back breaking than mowing lawns. But then I realized what we were doing. We weren't just mowing lawns…we were building something. We left every site looking way better than when we arrived. We were building big retaining walls and planting tree and shrubs. We were installing sod and spreading mulch. This was starting to get cool. This I could get used to. And the pay was better than it was for mowing lawns, so I was really starting to see that landscape construction was where I wanted to be.

I briefly attempted to work with Jimmy at that firewood and mulch yard in Lemont, Illinois that Jimmy and his brother were working at the day Jerry died. We were working for a man affectionately referred to as The Chief. The Chief's yard was a hell hole. Not a lick of shade anywhere to be found. The sun would beat down on us in a relentless manner all day. We spent our days lifting logs onto a log splitter to make firewood. It was exhausting work. The pay was miserable, the conditions were horrendous, and the hours were long. We came home wiped out every day. The usual stop on the way home was Nonno's Pizza on Ogden Avenue in Berwyn for a slice of pepperoni pizza and a can of orange pop, but Friday nights were burrito nights at El Faro. I couldn't get out of that job fast enough, so I quit. I just didn't want to deal with the mundane repetition of splitting wood all day. I needed a change.

After the brief stint with The Chief, and a couple summers of working construction with a few different companies, and continuing to head South every winter, I was asked if I would be interested in sticking around during the winter and becoming a plow truck driver. To be honest, the thought didn't thrill me, but with no Dead tour, the gulf coast winters were becoming more and more repetitive to me, so I gave it a shot. Those early snow plowing days of mine were some of the roughest. Companies wouldn't think twice about making an average plow route be 24-28 hours long. And that was for a normal snowfall. If we ever got a medium to large storm, we would watch the sun rise, and set again, three or four times before a shift ended. It took a toll on the body for sure. But it was good money, when it snowed, and it was allowing me to build deeper ties with companies for more year-round work. It was at this time that I decided to stop traveling, lay down some roots, and stick with landscaping year-round. It was time to settle down.

90

It wasn't long after I began plowing that I was moved up to Superintendent. Now I was no longer a working foreman, spreading mulch, laying sod, and digging holes. Now I was overseeing three to four crews that were performing those tasks. I was acting as the conduit between company and customer. This is where I really honed my craft for not only landscape construction management at a high level, but also crafted my skills in making connections across a variety of industries. During this stage of my career, my employers were sending to me to certification classes and continuing education seminars. I was building a body of work that was becoming more impressive with each passing year. As a result, my resume was looking really good to potential big-name employers. This afforded me the ability to work on some great projects as a Superintendent and Project Manager for companies like The Fisher Burton Company and Walsh Landscaping. The guidance and craft I learned with these companies, would eventually propel me to own my own landscape company one day.

In my two-decade career in the landscape industry, I was given the honor of working on some amazing and unique projects. One such project was when I was with The Fisher Burton Company, and it would prove to be a project I would never forget. We were contracted to handle the exterior set up for an event on Chicago's south side. I wasn't initially given much information about the project, and the talk surrounding it seemed like we were discussing something out of a spy novel. It was all very hush hush. I was entrusted with the projects management and I began attending the pre-construction meetings.

It was at this time that I discovered this was a birthday party for an extremely influential, and very eccentric Chicago millionaire. A production company from Hollywood was brought in to handle the event. This was shaping up to be something big. The project itself was almost indescribable. There would be a series of large venue tents in which the party goers would eat, drink, and dance the night away, and we were brought in to create an enchanted garden for party attendees to enjoy outside of the tent. It wasn't a true landscape project like you would think of. We were tasked with creating walking paths in the gravel lot, along which giant mounds of rock would be piled. There were cranes strategically placed throughout the enchanted garden that we decorated with various forms of plant life to make them look as if it was a post-apocalyptic world where nature had engulfed and overgrown the machines left behind. The cranes' arms held large evergreen trees that were

91

suspended in the air above the party goers' heads. This was, without a doubt, the most unique job I had ever been a part of.

The party was also set to have a big named musical act that was not disclosed to us. Once again, very hush hush. One day, while going over some of the projects details with my foreman, I heard some muffled music coming from inside the tent. I knew something was different that day as the already extremely tight security was even more ramped up than normal. The music stopped, and I carried on with my work. With all the construction noise, it was difficult to make out what the music was. Then it started again, only this time, the construction noise died down just long enough for me to realize that it was an Eagles song. Did they get an Eagles cover band to play the party? I walked into the tent to investigate further, and much to my surprise, there were The Eagles, performing a sound check on stage. I couldn't believe it. As I stood there in fandom amazement, they broke into "Rocky Mountain Way," and performed the whole song. I was in heaven. There were maybe thirty people total in the musical area of the tent, so we all had a front row seat. There I was, watching The Eagles perform, a mere ten feet in front of me…and all of this while I'm at work. All I could think to myself was "How many people get paid to watch The Eagles sing?" I immediately called my boss to tell him and held the phone up, so they could hear some of the sound check for themselves. I was as giddy as a school girl at a Beatles concert. At the end of that week, my boss printed out a fake copy of my pay stub which listed all the normal deductions, and then had one additional line of deductions that was equivalent to all of my take home pay. The deduction line read "Cost to see The Eagles up close." I still have that pay stub. I'll never forget that project as long as I live.

Another memorable project I worked on was many years before that, when I was working for a company called A Cut Above Landscaping. We were working on a mulch job in an affluent neighborhood in the southwest burbs. It seemed to be nothing special other than another rich man's house we were getting paid to making beautiful. The house sat on the curve of a road and there was severe lawn damage from where vehicles were constantly taking the curve too tight and veering off into the customers lawn. The transition from the curb line to the lawn was home to a rather steep ditch that took some skill to negotiate with a wheelbarrow loaded with mulch. On one trip back to the house with a fresh wheelbarrow of mulch, I mistimed my speed and ended up flipping the wheelbarrow, and myself, completely upside down, causing me to land square on my back. As I looked up, a man appeared before me and asked if I was OK. I said yes and began to get up to dust myself off. The man continued to speak, asking me if I could get any big rocks. At this point I was still paying more attention to myself, my embarrassment, and the fresh cut on my lower leg, than I was to the man speaking to me. So, I looked up to ask the man to repeat himself, and to my surprise I was standing in front of Blackhawks goalie, Eddie Belfour. It was his house we were working on. My mouth hit the floor. I wasn't a huge hockey fan, but EVERYBODY knew who Eddie The Eagle was, and here I was standing in his yard discussing his landscaping. I couldn't believe it. Big rocks? Sure thing, Eddie! Whatever you need, sir.

Another project I oversaw for Koch & Sons Landscaping was the installation of the new exterior exhibit for the giraffes, the exterior exhibit for the wild hogs, and the exterior exhibit for the wild dogs, at Lincoln Park Zoo. We were working with an international designer who specialized in designing zoo exhibits that were as similar to the animals' native lands while remaining safe. It was a fun, but irritating project. While we were a union shop, the unions in Chicago didn't recognize our suburban unions, so they began to make a beef against us. Before we knew it, they were threatening a shut down. The general contractor of the site worked it out with us to have us come in every day in the afternoon after the other trades went home for the day, and we would work all night long. The GC had flood lights brought in so we could work. It wasn't ideal, but it allowed us to continue working on the site. One of the weirdest parts of the experience was hearing the lion roar in the dead of night as you were walking through the zoo. Its roar could be felt in your rib cage. And while you knew he was in an enclosure, the hairs stood up on the back of your neck all the same because it was pitch black and you just never knew. I always walked a little quicker through the zoo after the sun had set, as if that would save me from an imminent lion attack.

On one end of the giraffe enclosure, there was a cluster of existing trees with a bare patch towards the back of the grove, near the wall that separated this exhibit from whatever exhibit was on the other side. We had to install a rather large tree that could only be moved into place by tying the canopy up, laying it on its side, and moving it in horizontally. Once moved into place, it had to be stood up, and then we had to gain access to the canopy to untie it. One of my crew members blurts out that he's on top of it, and he takes a ladder around the back of the exhibit wall. Knowing what I knew, I had to follow him, and bring the rest of the crew to see what was about to happen. The guy puts the ladder down into the moat of the enclosure that was behind the wall and begins to climb down. His intention is to climb down into the adjacent enclosure, then use the ladder to go up and over the wall to access the top of

93

the tree. It seemed like a lot of hassle to me, but I was at least willing to watch him try. What he didn't realize was that just because the enclosure we were working in was closed to animals, not every enclosure in the zoo was, and the enclosure he was currently climbing down into was one of the bear enclosures. He may not have realized it initially, but he got the message when he heard that bear let out a roar as he descended down the ladder. He may have set a new Midwest record for fastest ladder climb after gaining just a little bit of situational awareness that day.

In addition to these memorable projects, I've had the honor of working on unique and fun sites that include green roofs in both the downtown area as well as at Northwestern University, the new Silver Cross hospital in New Lenox, the new bear exhibits at Brookfield Zoo, as well as some really amazing high end residential properties throughout the Chicagoland area. I am really glad my career afforded me the chance to do some of things I've been able to do. One thing about landscaping that has always remained true throughout my career, it is anything but predictable. It's a career that always keeps you on your toes and allows your creative juices to flow. If you are a young person still trying to decide on a career path, I recommend you look into the horticulture industry.

During my time in the landscape industry, I have had the pleasure of getting to know some of the finest, hardworking people you'll ever meet, and a vast majority of them were Mexican immigrants, legal and illegal. The love these people have for their families, and the pride they take in their work, made my job an enjoyable experience for the better part of two decades. Many lunch breaks were spent with one of the crews, eating some damn fine homemade Mexican food. It was always the same from crew to crew...one man provided the camping grill and propane, one supplied the tortillas, and two or three men brought various meats, beans, and rice. We would grill our tortillas over the open flame and eat our tacos while swapping stories about life. Some of the best lunch breaks I've ever had were in a landscape trailer, sitting on a bucket, eating tacos with the guys. These were not criminals and rapists. They were hard working men who enjoyed the simple things in life. Many of these fine men reminded me of what I believed my immigrant grandfather was like. To each and every member of the Mexican immigrant community I've worked with, thank you for making my job easy, and enjoyable, for so long. I am honored to be able to call all of you my colleagues.

I will just conclude this chapter of the book by giving a specific shout out to Tom and Richard from The Fisher Burton Company. Above all other

94

companies I have ever worked for, they were the ones that taught me the most. They taught me the best practices for interpersonal relationships among trades as well as teaching me that the value of any one thing, in and of itself, may not be consequential to the overall value of the macro situation. In other words... don't complain to the customer about a thousand dollar extra he's asking for, free of charge, when the extra is on a two-million-dollar job from a company that provides us with six million a year in revenue. They taught me that the best employee in the world won't be a success at their job without the right tools and, more importantly, the right material. And above all, they taught me calm on the job. Not every situation is a world ending event. There are no problems, only solutions. The skills and lessons I learned at FBCO I took with me throughout the rest of my landscape career, and I still stay in touch with some of the people I worked with there. Tom and Richard, have a Tuesday slice of pizza and some cake for me. And you haven't lived until you witness an irritated and tired Kathy come into the office literally mumbling to herself about the various members of the human race she intends to impale as she makes her morning coffee. Thanks, guys. My time there was more than enjoyable.

"MY MOST BRILLIANT ACHIEVEMENT WAS MY ABILITY TO BE ABLE TO PERSUADE MY WIFE TO MARRY ME." – WINSTON CHURCHILL

CHAPTER NINE
Age, sex, underwear check, please

I know…hell of a title for a chapter, right? I'm guessing you're wondering what that title means. Back in the olden days of AOL, people would gather in sites called "chat rooms." And in the more generally social chat rooms, people would randomly type in "age, sex, location check please" to get an idea of who was in the chat. I would change that up, and send out an "age, sex, underwear check" request because, to be honest, I was in there looking for women. Everyone was at that time. It was the social hook up bridge between meeting someone in a bar, and the dating site age.

I didn't have a computer, but my cousin did, so he created an account for me, and I would hit the chat rooms while over at his place. I was The Lawn Doctor. And I was your typical, addicted chat room dork. Hours would be spent talking about absolutely nothing with strangers I would never meet. Until one day, someone responded to my ASU request, and we noticed that we had a Berwyn connection. After a little light chat room conversation, we then engaged in a private, instant message chat. I struggled a bit in the field of online chatting because my natural Kavorka doesn't come across a computer screen quite as strongly as it does face to face. The woman's name was Renee and we seemed to hit it off, so the private messaging led to actual phone conversations. This worked much better for me since I didn't need to be at my cousin's house hogging his computer. All I needed to do was give Renee my beeper number, and we could set up times to chat. Yeah…that's right…I said beeper. This was all before the era of smartphones, Facebook, and twitter. This was old school. And I had a great beeper. I had one of those see through beepers. Very hip. Man…the days of having a beeper on your belt. Seems like a hundred years ago.

After a few days of phone conversation, where I pegged the suave factor up to eleven, we went out on our first date. This was in May of 1997…which seems like a million years ago as I sit and write this today. I didn't have any real money to speak of, but I had just gotten paid, so I balled out. Dinner and a move? No problem. I got this. I swung my date through Bennigan's for a little dinner and charming conversation, and then it was off to a movie. I got this in the bag. What I didn't have, however, was the correct theatre for the movie we were going to see. Renee kept telling me that the theatre I was heading to was the wrong theatre, but that man-voice in my head kept telling me "She doesn't know what she's talking about. Stay the course. You got this, big guy." I was insistent that the theatre I drove to was the correct theatre, so I confidently walked up to the ticket window, date in arm, and asked for two tickets to "Austin Powers: Man Of Mystery." I was cool. I was suave. I had my A game working. I had the wrong damn theatre. I asked the ticket attendant if she was sure, as if somehow, she would turn around, realize she didn't know anything about the job she was doing, and save me from the embarrassment of turning to Renee without tickets. This was big. Not even to the movie portion of the first date, and I'm being proven wrong in real time. Awesome. So, with the full acceptance of my wrongness, I turned to my date to explain to her how I was sure this was the theatre, when she just smiled and asked me if I was ready to go to the right theatre now. That should've been her first red flag. Because of my insistence to prove my ignorance, we missed the first several minutes of the movie. My A game was looking to the bench to see if there were any players that could save this night.

But something must've gone right, because we went out again the following night. The first night's events tugged at the already frayed purse strings mightily, but I had enough to get me through to the following pay day. That was, of course, until date number two. In an attempt to redeem myself for the fiasco of the previous evening, and to show I was financially able to be in a relationship, I took Renee to Navy Pier. Once again, I just balled out. Didn't matter what it was or what it cost, I just made it happen. I redeemed myself. It was a good night. I knew that night that I was going to marry her. Now some may read that and think "Sure, it's easy to go back and claim that after being married all these years," but it's true, and Renee can confirm it, because I told her so that very night. I know...a little spooky to be told someone wants to marry you after only the second date, but I'm not an indecisive man and I know what I want, so I told her.

While Renee had her red flag warning in the form of my first date theatre fiasco, I had mine as well. Once, while hanging out at my apartment, I picked us up some dinner for the two of us. I asked Renee if she cared for chicken and she said yes. That's it. Not "this kind" of chicken or "that kind" of chicken, just "Yes...chicken sounds nice". So, I shot down to the KFC and grabbed a bucket of chicken. I like broasted chicken, so that is what I got. When I returned to the apartment, she looked at what I had returned with and gave it very un-enthusiastic "Oh...broasted chicken." I could tell this wasn't what she wanted. I told her I wasn't aware she didn't like that style of chicken and put my shoes on to retrieve the correct style of fowl for the evening's feast. She said no and told me it would be OK. So, I began to take my shoes off once again. As I bent over to untie my shoe, a comb hit the wall where my head was just seconds before. Now I swear to this day that the comb she hurled at me actually stuck in the wall, and she will tell you that's a lie, so I guess we will argue that event in our lives together until one of us is dead. That was a red flag I didn't heed. I mean, who throws a comb over chicken? Honestly.

The red flag I received that told me she was a handful was when she sprained her ankle visiting a potential side job with me. It was raining, and the customers deck was extremely slick, but the back yard was so nice, I wanted her to get out of the car and see it. She did and ended up doing a spin that would make most gymnasts envious and landed on the deck with a freshly sprained ankle. We obviously went to urgent care and she was given crutches and told to stay off her feet for a while. So, what does Renee do? She goes to Venture and hobbles through the store picking up books, snacks, and anything else she needed for an extended stay at home, completely defying the doctor's orders.

What I didn't know about Renee was that, at that time, she was going through a divorce from the man she dated through much of her high school years. She wanted to date and experience the lifestyle she didn't get to have since she had been with the same man for so long. I had been trekking across the country, partying my ass off and was looking to settle down. We wanted different things and I wasn't what she wanted at that point in her life. Sure, I was fun to be around, devilishly handsome, and had a severe case of the Kevorka, but Renee still wasn't ready to settle down. So, she kept dating and disappeared from my life for the better part of six weeks. At this point I had written her off. Until one night when I was out with my cousin and some friends at a club in Palatine, Illinois. There I am having some drinks when the beeper goes off. I call the number and it's Renee. Out of the blue. Without warning. It had to be the Kavorka. She asked where I was and then came to club to see me. We hung out that night and began dating regularly the next day. Throughout it all though, she insisted on not being exclusive. She had been tied down and now wanted to be free. This caused a lot of friction in our relationship that first year. It damn near drove me insane. We were just on different pages.

Because Renee wanted to date, and I didn't, Renee insisted I go out with other women in an attempt to hold me at bay in regard to settling down. During that time, I met some real doozies. One girl told me, within the first five minutes of our date, that she had four kids by four men and that she was only looking to get pregnant with number five. That was going to be a hard pass from me. Seriously? What is wrong with people? It was a string of first dates with troglodyte after troglodyte, each one of them more useless than the last. At one point in time I thought there was absolutely no hope for the human race.

Another girl I dated turned out to be a story we still tell to this day. I had met this girl through a dating service. When we initially spoke on the phone, it was amazing. She had a smoky, raspy kind of soft bedroom voice that drove me nuts. I had to meet this woman. She would schedule her time for our phone conversations around her time in the bath, and I could hear the water gently splashing about in the background. I had to meet this woman. Our phone conversations lasted for some time before we actually met in person. We would talk for hours, even though I mainly just listened silently to that smoky voice of hers. It was becoming tattooed on my brain. I had to meet this woman. We finally planned to meet at a bar in the northwest suburbs. Renee had a girl's night out planned, so off we went on our separate ways for the evening. When I arrived at the bar, I had a beer and asked the bartender if she had been in yet. She told me she was a regular there and that the bartender knew her. After a short wait, and a couple primer beers, I heard that voice. It was her. She was behind me asking if I was Tom. That voice. I had to meet her. As I turned around, I discovered that she was in a wheelchair. It was a bit of a shock considering she never mentioned that she was in a wheelchair. I grabbed another beer and followed her to the pool table area as she wanted to play a game. As we sat and drank, she explained to me that she had been in an accident and was paralyzed from the waist down, but that she still functioned on her own. I continued to drink trying to figure out a way to tell her that she needs to let prospective suitors know that she's in a wheelchair, without being my typical rude self about it. The worst part was that she was whoopin' my ass at that pool table. After a few hours of her schooling me in the game of pool, and me increasing my drinking as each hour passed, I was pretty sloppy and in need of a ride. She called the usual cab company she frequented to get around, and I paged Renee. After several attempts at paging her, I called the restaurant she was at. When I finally got Renee on the phone, she asked me how the date was going. I explained that I was pretty drunk and that my date was in a wheelchair. "What did you do to her?!?!" is what I heard back on the other end of the phone? I replied "Me??? No…she came that way. I didn't do a damn thing to her. She's paralyzed from the waist down. Now come and get me, please…. I'm hammered." Evidently Renee and her girlfriends got quite the belly laugh when Renee returned to the table and recounted the phone conversation with me. It was, by far, the single weirdest date I have ever been on in my entire life. Ladies…if you're in a wheelchair, that's something that must be disclosed ahead of time. It isn't a deal breaker by any means, but can be a shock to the system if not known ahead of time.

Towards the end of our first year together, I had enough. I had been a string of horrible dates, and if I was going to be miserable, I might as well be miserable alone. I told her to leave my apartment and that I was done with her. I then took a shower and got ready to head out for a bit, only to find Renee still in the stairwell. She told me she wanted to be with me and asked me what she could do to prove she wanted a relationship with me, so I told her to get us an apartment together and that would prove she meant it. She went right out and got us our first place together. To be honest, I would've still dated her without that first apartment, but I knew it was the one way I could get her to settle down with me, so I played the hand in front of me.

That first place was a little one-bedroom apartment in Roselle, Illinois on the second floor. We had a little balcony and a very small kitchen, but it did the trick. We had absolutely no furniture. Our bed/couch was a futon, and we had a very old TV on top of a laundry basket. We got a kitchen table and chairs from relatives. We couldn't even host a dinner if we wanted to, but man did we have some fun in that place. Eventually we pieced together some living room furniture and splurged on a king size bed. We even had a real Christmas tree that first year. I was doing some landscape jobs on the side but didn't have a garage or trailer to keep tools in, so the coat closet immediately to your right as you entered the apartment was filled with landscape tools, including a backpack blower. How Renee tolerated that is still beyond me. On Halloween we would hang declarations on the railing around the balcony. There was exactly enough room for one chair and a Weber grill on that balcony, which was all we really needed at the time. In time, we even bought a desk and computer that was housed in our bedroom. For someone that had spent the past several years living in a tent, this was high end for me. Especially that king sized bed. Are you kidding? I'm really laying my body down on a king size bed every night? Wow.

The other tenants in the apartment building pretty much kept to themselves. There was a small pool we maybe swam in once. The laundry was down in the basement, so lugging everything up and down was a bit of a pain, but you struggled through it. Groceries were always the big thing. There was no way we were making that trip twice. A second-floor apartment is an automatic one-tripper with the groceries. We would grab Yu's Chinese food for takeout whenever we could swing it, and I quickly developed a relationship with the local pizza guy. We even had Jimmy living with us for a brief period. We had some good memories in that apartment.

When I said Jimmy came to live with us, yes, I mean that Jimmy. He had just gotten out of jail...I know, you're shocked...and needed a place to stay. The company I was working for at the time, Grant & Power Landscaping, was looking to bring on more people, so I arranged an interview. Jimmy got the job and the deal was as follows: he wouldn't have to pay for gas to and from work, but he had to give us half his money every week. We were going to use half of what he gave us on bills and groceries, and we would save the other half of what he gave us, so he had a nice bundle of money heading into the offseason in December. He crashed on the couch and pitched in around the house. Late at night he would borrow my portable CD player and listen to tunes until he passed out. He lasted two weeks before he screwed us on that deal. He got his first paycheck and told us he was going to hop the train back to Cicero to see a few old friends that Friday night. He would cash his check while he was out there and bring us the money when he returned. He returned at 4:00am Monday morning, broke. I had to tell him he wasn't welcome here anymore. I had a relationship now...I wasn't playing the old games anymore. I wanted more out of life. Jimmy just wanted to party. We were on different pages. As much as that pained me to do to a man I had spent so much time traveling with, at some point, you just have to grow the hell up.

While Renee and I were dating in those early years, we were obviously able to get a lot more often. We really had some good times during those pre-children years. Our Sunday morning trips to Omega for breakfast were awesome. Cream of chicken soup and saganaki were my Sunday staples. One night, we were out at a bar in the city called Hang Up's. It was a relatively unique place in that its main floor was more of a dance vibe, while the basement level was a classic rock kind of scene. On this particular night, we were there with my cousin, Joey, and several of his friends. One of the men in attendance, Shane, had planned to propose to his girlfriend by fixing it so she won a giveaway at the bar. That giveaway would be a box that contained clue after clue of what was to come, with the ring being the last item pulled from the box. Renee was in rare form. She was out, she was

102

young, she was carefree…she was getting hammered. She kept buying rounds of shots, only to find that the guys weren't paying attention when the shots were lined up on the bar, so she would end up doing all the shots. Then the guys would turn around, ask what happened to their shot, so Renee would line up another round and do a shot with them. So, for every one shot the guys were doing, Renee was doing two. Folks, believe me when I tell you that girlfriend was HAMMERED. It's the kind of hammered that makes bartenders question their life's work. The kind of hammered that requires you to rehearse how to order more drinks, because your coherency level left you ten shots ago. The kind of hammered that makes one's father proud, and frightened, all at the same time. Getting her back to the car was harder than a left turn downtown. It was only a short walk to the parking garage, but then it was up the spiral parking structure, making her more and more unbalanced with every step. Once I was able to corral her into the car, I headed out of the city along 290 west. As we headed out of town, like a toddler two minutes into a road trip, Renee declared she must use the bathroom. I exited the highway and found a gas station. Renee stumbled into the establishment like someone who had just been whacked upside the head with a cast iron skillet and used the bathroom. I don't know exactly how long she was in that bathroom, but I'm pretty sure I could've gotten an outpatient medical procedure done during my wait. Just as I was about to go in and see if my date was still alive, out came Renee. She had entered a bathroom stall, pulled her pants down, and in doing so, fell forward against the door. She then mustered all her strength to push herself off of the door, safely falling back onto the toilet. A solid recovery. But there was one small problem…she was too drunk to figure out how to stand up. That's what she was doing in there…trying to remember how to stand up. Have YOU ever been so hammered you forgot how to stand up? My date reached that state on intoxication without me having to buy her shot.

Renee turned to me one night in 1999 and said, "Do you have any plans for May 7th?" I said no, and she informed me that she didn't either, and maybe that would be a good day to get married. Married? But I can't afford a wedding. I knew I wanted to get married, but I also knew I could never afford the kind of wedding she deserved. But she didn't care about that. She already had a big wedding with the gown and limo and hall full of friends. She just wanted to head to the courthouse and make it legal. I was OK with that, but all these years later, it's the biggest regret of mine from our early years together. I wish I had the resources to give her a big wedding and nice honeymoon. Instead we had a courthouse wedding, grabbed some Portillo's chocolate cake and hit the road for a weekend in Bloomington, Indiana.

Yeah…you read that right…we honeymooned in Bloomington, Indiana, and we had a blast. We spent a little time in my home town of Linton and was able to spend a little quality time with family. So, we tied the knot on May 7th, 1999. Almost two years exactly after we first met, in a small courthouse ceremony attended by my father and step-mother, her parents, her sister, Lisa, and her sister, Michelle. While we were awaiting our turn to be called, Jo recognized someone that worked there. Leave it to Jo to know someone everywhere she went. And, of course, she was able to get us bumped up as result. I stood there, sweating my giblets off, damn near ready to puke. I knew this was what I wanted, but there I was…after years on the road literally hitchhiking across the country and sleeping in a tent, about to get married. Jesus, Mary, and Joseph…are you sure you want to do this?! Yeah…I did want to.

The wedding itself almost didn't happen. The day before the wedding, I was rushing to finish a side job and the guy working with me was sick. This caused Renee to be called into action. The only problem was that both Renee and I were also sick. We spent the entire day before our wedding installing bullet block edging and mulch at a customer's house, while vomiting at will in his yard. It was a long, brutal day. I honestly didn't even know if we would be physically able to make our own wedding.

After a short period of time in the apartment, including one New Year's blizzard that saw my sister-in-law snowed in with us for a couple days, and also saw her tear through every last scrap of food in the house, and even more that was ordered in, we moved into the house Renee grew up in on Ruby Street in Franklin Park, Illinois. It was one of a few houses that her extended family on her father's side owned, and they allowed us to live there. It was a big, old house. Great character. A four-bedroom, two story house with all the old school aspects of a near west suburban Chicago home. I didn't care for the fact that it didn't have air conditioning, and the radiator heat would burn my knees in the bathroom, but it had its up sides. It sat in three lots of land, so the side and back yard was huge for an urban lot. One entire lot was a gravel driveway from street to alley. You could park fifteen cars there easily. The first floor consisted of a half bath, kitchen, living room, dining room, and office. There was a covered front porch and an enclosed back stairwell that led you to an extremely creepy unfinished basement, complete with old coal stage rooms. The upstairs contained four bedrooms, and a full bathroom with a claw foot tub. This house had the bones of being something great. The garage was actually a very old chicken coop. It was failing and leaning and really should have been torn down. With a little money, and a lot of elbow grease, that house could have been marvelous.

It was while we were in this house that our three dogs got out when the gate was left open one day. The police returned two of the dogs, but Moose, our German Shepard mix, still hadn't been located. As we came around the front of the house, we saw Moose. He was barreling down the middle of Ruby Street, in full gallop run, with a Franklin Park cop right behind him. Moose took a sharp left turn into the driveway and then another into the back yard. The cop came into the driveway fast and gave it the old hockey skate stop. Moose had been outrunning him for blocks. The officer was rather impressed. Moose would have made a great Dead tour dog.

This was also the house where we almost lost George. George was black and white kitten of some outdoor cats that Renee had brought home years before we met. He was everything to Renee. While living in Franklin Park, we made a cat bed for George between the toilet and the wall in the downstairs bathroom where he loved to sleep. Every morning I would go to the bathroom and he would awaken from his sleep when I entered the room. A couple days went by where he didn't wake up. I just figured he was tired. Around the third day, it suddenly hit me that not only has he not woken up, but he hasn't moved. So, one night I gently nudged his head with my foot, and his head just flipped to one side and then over. He wasn't moving. Something was wrong. Renee freaked. We soon found ourselves at the 24-hour emergency vet in town. They took George back and examined him while Renee paced the floor of the waiting room. A few minutes later we were called back. They had George in a giant sink with some god awful smelling chemical being rubbed into his fur. They then had us watch while they rinsed him off, and thousands of fleas just rained down from his body. He had gotten outside at some point and got fleas. Because he was an indoor cat, and the dogs had flea treatments, we didn't think to treat him. The doctors showed us how white his gums were from being almost sucked dry. We were informed that had he gone another day, he'd be dead. He needed blood. Renee didn't have a spending limit to save George's life, so we told the doc to do whatever it took. That turned into a nice little $1,500.00 vet bill. Yeah…that's right…we paid $1,500.00 to give a cat a blood transfusion. It still baffles me.

Renee's mother, Diane, would eventually get remarried to Mike. Mike and Cracker, as Diane is known, would eventually find themselves the grandparents of ten grandchildren over a sixteen-year period. Magnolia, Ayden, Riley, Reese, Lily, Charlotte, Devin, Tommy, Gage, and the newest member of the family, Jaxon, would become the lineage of the Fuentes family. While I have had my share of really bad experiences with step parents, that is not the case with Mike. Mike has been a tremendous grandfather to my children and is the favorite of the younger kids by a mile. He's the grandpa with the fart machine who tracks Santa for you on Christmas Eve. He's Popi. He's great. As is everyone in my new extended family that Renee brought me into. Renee is the oldest of three girls. Her sisters have been an instrumental part of our families' lives. Michelle and Lisa are godmother to Maggie and Lily, and I couldn't imagine my children's lives without them. Renee's family extends out into a large web of cousins, aunts and uncles that can certainly fill a house for a birthday party. To know the Violet clan is to know her aunt and uncle, Lamar and Nancy. Two true characters. Nancy would hop on a plane and come get you in the middle of the night if you truly needed her to, just don't use any foul language around her. And if you're taking a trip with Uncle Lamar, bring a snack, because he never uses the highway. But you will be entertained for your entire journey, because nobody has more tales than Lamar. His stories are the stuff of legend. Lamar and Nancy had three daughters, Sherrill, Suzanne, and Leigh Anne. Those three daughters have gone on to give Lamar and Nancy nine grandchildren and four great grandchildren so far. Like I said, it's a good sized extended family. Renee has since lost her fair share of people as well. Aunt Marla, whose son, Jimmy now lives in Tennessee with his own wife and daughter, was a familiar face at every family event and bingo game. Aunt Dorothy, or Auntie, was a wonderful woman I am proud to have gotten to know before she left us. Just a no-nonsense, old school woman who could bake you a pie, knit you a sweater, or grab you by the ear if you screwed up. And Grandma Martha was truly the matriarch of the family. Her face was a well-known one in the history of Franklin Park. And the list goes on. Grandma Jean, Carin, Cari, Grandma Rose, Aunt Darlene....the family is extensive. And we would soon add to that large family ourselves.

Tom Powell Jr.

"HAVING CHILDREN REALLY CHANGES YOUR PRIORITIES." – CINDY CRAWFORD

CHAPTER TEN
The pitter patter of little feet and putting down roots where the waters meet

May 16th, 2001. That is the date our first child was born. Magnolia Lynn Powell came into the world via c-section after torturing her mother through hours of excruciating labor. It was the culmination of a long journey trying to get pregnant while fighting around Renee's PCOS. When setting out to start our family, we discovered Renee couldn't get pregnant without medical assistance. Some of that assistance was administered in a doctor's office, and some was administered at home. Never in all my years did I think I would find myself sitting on the edge of a bed trying to make myself stick a needle in my wife, so I could administer what she needed to help her get pregnant. My whole life was spent fearing I was going to accidentally get someone pregnant, and here I was with this needle in my hands, trying to get someone pregnant on purpose. Life comes at you fast. But, after struggling, and trying, and endless doctor's visits, we finally had our first child...a daughter.

She was named Magnolia by me after my favorite flower from the Merrill Magnolia tree, and after the Grateful Dead song "Sugar Magnolia." Her name did not come without controversy, and didn't come to pass without one major league, all time asshole move by me. As I presume many young, expecting parents do, we created lists of our favorite names. To me, naming a child is one of the most important things you will ever do as a human. You're

109

choosing what another person will be called forever. My list contained several odd and off beat names. I know…you're shocked. Atop my list for boys was Vlad, Sebastian, Luke, Tommy, and Garry. My list of girl's names were all flowers. I love flower names for girls. There's something so classic about it. And given my chosen career, flower names just seemed to fit. Renee wasn't a fan of many of them. Iris? Nope. Violet? Not happening. But I stood firm on Magnolia. Renee gave me the old "OK, we'll come back to that", and we moved our focus on to the boy's names. Vlad? You want to name a kid Vlad? That was pretty much the response to the top boy name on my list. Of course, I wanted a Vlad. Vlad Caleb Powell…that's a powerful name. At the time, Renee really liked Jacob Alexander. I tried my best to explain to her that if we send a boy to school with the initials J.A.P. we had better start karate lessons at a very early age, because he was going to need to know how to throw some hands. So, we debated, and we waited and then came the ultrasound. It's a boy! Really? A son right out of the gate? That was always my dream. Give me twenty little girls but give me one son right out of the gate. Hot damn! Now we needed to narrow down on those boy names. We agreed to pick a girl's name, in the off chance the ultrasound was incorrect. It seemed like the safe move. Given the certainty of the technician, Renee felt safe in agreeing to Magnolia Lynn. After all, it's a boy. No need to worry. When the next child is a girl, you can once again fight for Elizabeth Diane. As the discussions wore on, I eventually agreed to Jacob Alexander. One day we were called in for an emergency ultrasound very late in the pregnancy. As the technician performed the ultrasound, she asked us if we knew the sex. We said we did, and the tech then asked us if we had a name picked out for her. Her? I'm sorry…did you say "her"? I think you're looking at the wrong screen. There's a boy in there. The tech corrected me and sent us home now wondering what we were going to be having. The room is already blue and there's already a football in there…it has to be a boy. Nope. "Congratulations…it's a girl!" Huh? Back to the naming process now. When the nurse eventually brought the paperwork around for the name, it hit us both again that we had agreed to Magnolia, which Renee only agreed to because we were told we were having a boy. So, I grabbed the pen, looked at Renee and said, "Magnolia Lynn, right?" "Let's talk about this," was her reply. I didn't know what there was to talk about. We agreed to this name. But Renee didn't like the name at the time and wanted to try to change my mind. I was pissed. And that's when I pulled the most shameful, asshole move I've pulled on that woman. I tossed the paperwork and the pen onto the hospital tray, as she held the baby, and told her to give me call when she figured out what she wanted the baby to be called. I wasn't participating. And I walked out. How that woman didn't kill me with the nearest surgical equipment is still a mystery to me. Eventually Renee would relent, and our first child would officially be named Magnolia Lynn Powell.

Holy shit...I'm someone's dad! How did that happen? Are we really sure I'm qualified to be responsible for another human being? While Magnolia was a great child from the moment she got home, her entrance into the world was anything but drama free. As I mentioned earlier, Renee labored for hours with Maggie. It was a rough ride. Her mother and I were there, but it was up to Renee to do all the heavy lifting. At one point, my mother-in-law asked me if I wanted to go down to the cafeteria and grab a quick bite to eat. We asked Renee if it was OK and she said yes. Upon our return to the delivery room, we noticed that Renee's father had arrived, and Renee's water had broken. Renee was also in the process of telling her father that her mother and I abandoned her and that she had no clue where we were. Like I said, it wasn't an easy day for Renee. The doctors put a monitor on Maggie's head, which was attached to a cord that led to a screen. When they took Renee in for the c-section, I stayed out and her mother accompanied her. I was a bit of a basket case and there was no way I was going to be able to be in a room with someone who was cutting my wife open. When they opened Renee up, and began removing Maggie, the cord was still attached, so it began to dig into Renee. She let out a scream we could hear from the waiting area. Without even thinking, I popped up and hit the button to open the automatic doors which led to the surgical area. You know...the area I'm not supposed to enter. As the doors opened, and I began to dash in, my father-in-law grabbed me by the shirt, slammed me up against the wall, and held me there while he explained to me that she was in a room full of doctors and nurses and there was nothing I was going to be able to contribute. He probably saved me a whole heap of trouble that day. A short while later, my mother-in-law emerged with my daughter...and raced past all of us on her way to the nursery. The doctor had told her she could take the baby, with a nurse, to the nursery, and she took that task literally. So, my first glimpse of Magnolia was as she was bundled up in a receiving blanket and flying past me at mach two. But you know what...that grandma would still do anything to keep her Maggie safe. Our kids have been lucky to have the kind of extended family support they get, from both sides of their family. It was later that day that I got to hold my daughter for the first time. I was still in disbelief that someone was allowing me to be a father. After all, I was the high school dropout carney who followed the Grateful Dead and got laid off every winter. But there I was, holding my child. She was perfect. Absolutely perfect. And I didn't do it the way my parents did it. I had a relationship where both parties wanted kids. I had learned from my parents' mistakes.

During Renee's stay in the hospital, she began to get cabin fever. She just wanted to be able to walk around a bit, feel the sun on her face and smell the fresh air. She was bouncing off the walls. When we left the hospital, Renee just couldn't stand the thought of heading straight home and subsequently being locked up in the house for the foreseeable future with a newborn, so we visited my father and step-mother. We stayed there for over eight hours. And Maggie slept damn near the whole time. We now say that this is what contributed to Maggie being someone who is always on the go now. Eventually we made it home and introduced Maggie to her blue bedroom and football. God damn ultrasound techs! I never believed another ultrasound tech after Maggie.

Magnolia was the first grandchild for either of Renee's parents, the first for my father, and the second for my step-mother. She received the lion's share of attention early and often. We named Renee's sister, Michelle, as her godmother, and my father as her godfather. After all, the old man was always there for me. I was damn sure he would always be there for his grandkids. And Michelle has proven to always be there for her nieces and nephews. We made the correct choices. The families showered her with everything and showed her a very loved childhood. But she would soon be sharing that spotlight with a little sister.

September 29th, 2004. That's the day our second child was born. Lily Marie Powell was born via c-section like her sister, with the slight change being that this time it was a scheduled procedure. No labor. As you can guess, this made for a much smoother time for Renee. And, once again, I didn't go into the delivery room, my mother-in-law did. Look, I know it's a common medical procedure done by a professional. I get it. But if I see someone cut my wife open, my reflex is to drop them like a sack o' taters, so it was just best that I be detached from the situation. I sat in a small, dimly lit waiting area with some family members. Waiting. Ugh...the waiting sucks. I don't like to wait. There is shit to do, so there's no time to wait. Let's go. Chop chop. Since Renee's sister, Michelle, was already named godmother to Magnolia, we had informed Renee's other sister, Lisa, she would be the godmother to this child, so natural she was also in attendance, eagerly awaiting news of her new god child. I specifically remember her being there because when I wouldn't go back to the delivery area with the nurse to see Renee and the baby until the nurse told me the sex of the baby, Lisa jumped in the air and shouted with excitement when we were told it was a girl. I remember this because I wanted a son, so I shot her a side eye in response to her celebration. It

112

wasn't her fault. She was excited. But I knew Renee and I probably wouldn't have another child, so this was my last chance at a son, and now that chance was gone. I was salty.

Saltiness aside, however, I had a daughter to meet. This time I was able to see her in the delivery room, rather than racing away to the nursery. Lily was so small. Perhaps the fact that I now had a three-year-old attached to our hips is why this little baby looked as small as she seemed. Lily Marie, by the way, is the only one of the kids' names that Renee didn't fight me over. She was a Lily…it just fit. So now the garden was filling out. We had a Magnolia and a Lily. I was happy. It was time to go home and introduce Lily to the world. World…Lily. Lily…world. Ok, let's do this.

Once again Renee and I battled to get pregnant, but we had been through that fight before. We knew what to expect. This time we were also much more prepared to leave the hospital with a baby. Pfft…. we're veterans at this game now. We got this. Maggie and Lily shared a room in the beginning. They've always had a close bond, even to this day, even though Lily would scream while Maggie was just trying to get some sleep. Lily was, shall we say, a tad fussier as an infant. Man, could that kid scream. For such a small baby, she had some above average lungs. Lily would come to be called Bean because of her bean shaped image on the ultrasound. Bean was a perfect match with Maggie. Now that our family was complete, it was time to find our own home, and a community we wanted to raise a family in. After all, these girls should have their own rooms.

I was hired to run the landscape installation of a large site in Shorewood, Illinois, so we began our search around that area. I would take rides around lunch time through the back-country roads, and I eventually found myself in Minooka, Illinois. It seemed like a nice little town. It had some shops, a few places to eat, and it had, at the time, a ton of new houses going up. There was one red flag that stood out to me, however. One day I stopped in to the local Arby's for lunch and when I asked the young woman taking my order if she lived in the town, she said that she indeed did live in Minooka. So, I asked he what her thoughts were on the town, and she replied with; "Oh, I think it's great. We hardly have any niggers or nothin'." Wow. I was speechless. Initially I thought maybe Minooka was not a place to be settling down in if racism was so freely exhibited there. But, you will run in to racists anywhere, and we have come to learn that racism is not the norm around here. After poking my head around the town for a few weeks during my lunch breaks, I told Renee about it and we began to research houses in that area. The houses seemed affordable, and the area seemed safe enough, so we began to line up a list of houses we wanted to see.

During one of my excursions looking for potential houses, I made a turn down a road I hadn't been on before, and I wound up in Channahon, Illinois. After checking my map, I realized this town was just as geographically desirable as Minooka was, so I began digging into what this town was all about. Turns out it was basically just like Minooka. They shared high schools and the park district, and were basically one big town, so we lined up some house we wanted to see in Channahon as well. We really didn't know much about either town, so we were really rolling the dice and hoping for the best. Given how far away we lived, we had to be strategic when scheduling showings, so we scheduled a full Saturday of house viewings. We managed to get all the viewings in during one sweeping effort. For weeks I had dreamed about seeing one particular split level, so I made sure we scheduled that last. I wanted to end with a bang. I talked that house up so big, I was absolutely convinced that it was going to be our house. This house had a lot of work that needed to be done to it, but it sat on a huge corner lot, and land is never something you can upgrade, so I really wanted that house. At the last minute we found another house right around the corner, so I agreed to tack that one into the end of our day, but I was certain we were buying the split level. As with the movie theatre on our first date, I was wrong. When we viewed the last add-on house, Renee didn't have to take ten steps into the dwelling before she blurted out "This is the house we're buying." Excuse me? What did you say? I don't think I heard you quite right. But I heard it loud and clear at the signing table. It was a three-bedroom, bath and a half ranch in a quiet neighborhood that was a little older than all of the new construction neighborhoods in town. It had a one car garage, a run-down fence and shed, and tremendously horrible landscaping. The house had some miles on it, but it was now ours. Finally, our OWN home.

And in such a great town, too. Channahon sits where interstates 80 and 55 meet in the far southwest suburbs of Chicago. Its name is Potawatomi for "meeting of the waters," because it is where the Des Plaines river and the DuPage river converge to form the Illinois river. As you can imagine, this results in a lot of water recreation possibilities at your fingertips. It has a great school system that we couldn't be happier with. Channahon School district 17 is run so well, it runs a surplus every year and recently rebated back to each citizen a third of their property taxes. Did YOU get a third of your property taxes back one month before Christmas? If not, there are plenty of lots available to build your home on right here in Channahon. My kids have had very good luck with the teachers they've been assigned, but hands down their favorite faculty member is the bus driver, Mrs. Carver. In addition to the amazing schools, we have a great park district. The park district here boasts tons of soccer, baseball, and softball fields, a top scale gym and fitness center, indoor facilities for every activity, a full golf course, and the Tomahawk Aquatic Center, featuring a zero-depth entry pool and two water slides. We have hiking trails, controlled industrial growth, very low crime, and a plethora of great small businesses. The town is a bit more conservative than I would like, so I'm a bit out of place, being the unabashed liberal that I am, but we work around that. And they have a great taco joint! Taco Burrito King has now become my local taco provider, and they are responsible for satisfying my taste buds on many a night since we've moved to town. If you do not live near enough to a good taco joint, you should move. You don't need that kind of negativity in your life.

While looking in Channahon, the prices were affordable, the taxes were low, and it was close to work. It was perfect. It still is perfect. Over our many years in Channahon, we've been heavily involved in their park districts programs, and we couldn't be happier with the way the town is run. We've raised our children, enjoyed the abundance of outdoor space in town, and set down roots that I hope our children will carry on in their adult lives. I love it here. It's the perfect mixture of small town atmosphere and steady, intelligent growth. I fully intend to spend the rest of my life here. GO INDIANS!

But buying the house wasn't as simple as a marathon session of signing your name and then writing a large check…at least not for us. We were buying the house from a single father in his early twenties who had a three-year-old son and getting him and his lawyer to respond to correspondences was like pulling teeth. As we would learn…AT THE CLOSING TABLE…he hadn't made a mortgage payment in eighteen months and had gone into foreclosure just a few days before the closing. We couldn't close on the house because the bank wanted another ten thousand dollars from someone. The seller thought we should increase our down payment by ten grand to cover what the bank wanted. And since that was the single dumbest thing I have ever heard of in my entire life, we refused. But now we were in a really bad spot. Because we had made an offer, and it was accepted, and we had a closing date set, we already set the wheels in motion to move our lives down there. Renee had taken a job in Channahon and we arranged in-home daycare for our three-year-old and newborn daughters, with someone we didn't know. We knew exactly zero people in town and now we couldn't close on the house. This began a rather exhausting period where Renee was traveling from Franklin

Park to Channahon very early every morning, dropping our kids off at a daycare we didn't know, and returning with them in the evening, often not walking in the door until eight or nine at night. This wasn't going to work. It simple wasn't sustainable. I was in phone calls daily, sometimes hourly, with lawyers and real estate agents trying to get this deal closed. In the meantime, we kept looking, but we really weren't finding anything that fit our family. After many days of arguments, I finally reached out to the seller's lawyer directly to see if there was anything that could be done. I would learn that he was sympathetic to our cause because he hadn't yet been paid by his client and was just as upset about the entire situation as we were. As our lawyers and the banks worked everything out, the seller's lawyer agreed to let us move into the house as renters, until we could work out a deal to close on the house. We paid him a one-time payment of $1500, which covered the money he didn't get from his client, and we lived in the house, off of that one rent payment, for a little over three months while all of the suits worked out a deal. It still wasn't ideal because we didn't want to unpack everything, but it reduced Rennes travel time by nearly an hour and a half...each way. The phone calls and debating raged on. I would call to see if we were any closer to a deal, the lawyers would tell me we weren't, and the bank still wanted another ten grand from us, and I would proceed to tell them to go pound salt and hang up on them. This went on for weeks. I simply refused to cover the seller's debt. After much arguing, and uncounted phone calls, we finally were able to come to an agreement and close on the house and begin making it ours. The bubble had burst, and banks were foreclosing at an astronomical rate, and they simply did not want yet another foreclosed house to sit on.

This house now holds our family's memories. This is the house I finally got to watch my beloved Indianapolis Colts win the city's first Super Bowl championship, and witness Peyton Manning hoist the Lombardi trophy over his head. It's where we witnessed the Cubs clinch the World Series in game seven. We've hosted birthday parties and holiday gatherings here. We've changed and remodeled the house a few times, and everyone has shuffled from one bedroom to another at one point in time. We have marks in the door jams showing the kids growth, and there's a story about one event or another in every corner. This is our home. My kids didn't have to suffer the kind of instability I had as a child. They went to school in the same town they lived in. They had friends in the same neighborhood they lived in. They were building memories I couldn't. I did it. I made my kids' lives better than what I had. THAT is a pretty good damn feeling. Our family was set. Life was perfect. Life, it turns out, was getting ready to throw us some curveballs that Anthony Rizzo couldn't hit.

116

December 1st, 2011. That's the day our third child was born. Tommy Lee Powell III was born, as his sisters were, via c-section. Once again, it was a scheduled procedure. Unlike with his sisters, however, he wasn't planned. In fact, Renee and I had already made the decision not to have any more kids, so the lad really snuck up on us. After not being able to get pregnant the first two times, Renee suddenly got pregnant naturally. She woke me up very early on a Saturday to tell me this news, to which I told her to stop joking and let me sleep. As she turned to leave the room, I could see she was crying, so I knew there was more to it than just a joke. This might be real. Could it be real? There no way it's real! Yep...it's real. She had a feeling that perhaps she was pregnant for a few days, so she bought a bunch of home pregnancy tests, and had already done a few of them by the time she decided to wake me up with life altering news. I made her do another one as I couldn't believe what I was hearing. Sure enough, she was pregnant. What the hell were we going to do now? Our kids were well along in age and we had become comfortable enough in our decision not to continue to have kids, that we were getting used to not having the bottles and the diapers and the teething. It was relaxing. We just had a talk about what we're going to do with all of the day care money we would be saving once Lily would no longer need to attend. I've said it before, and I'll say it again...life comes at you fast. We were literally starting all over again. In fact, earlier that week I gave away the last baby item that remained from Lily, her stroller. That was it. We had nothing in the house for a baby's arrival. We were screwed. And, as you can guess, it was my fault. I was tasked with getting a vasectomy once we decided we were done having kids. Given the fact that Renee couldn't get pregnant naturally, and I was vehemently opposed to someone cutting open my sack, I never got the procedure. When it comes to my body, I live by two steadfast rules....my asshole is exit only, and I never let anyone cut into my twig and berries. Beyond that, it's all up for grabs. Hey, it has worked for me so far, so why rock the boat now, right? This would end up being a decision I would never hear the end of. Every time that boy is unruly and throwing a fit, I am reminded that I didn't get the vasectomy. I would bet good money that Renee ends up having my headstone engraved with "Here lies Tom Powell Jr. The man who didn't get the vasectomy he said he would get."

When the lad was born, I decided to go into the delivery room. I was hoping for a boy, knowing that we were going to make sure this didn't happen again through surgical solutions, so I wanted to do everything different than I did with the girls. After all, everything else was different about this pregnancy, why not take it all the way? The first two were planned, this one wasn't. The first two required medical assistance to achieve pregnancy, this one happened naturally. Renee even felt different. And this time, we went the extra mile and had a 3D ultrasound scan with a long history of being correct when they tell you the sex of the baby. They told us it was a boy, and even sitting in front of a doctor who is almost never wrong, I blurted out "I still don't believe you. I just don't believe you." Being inside the delivery room was, hands down, one of the weirdest experiences of my life. Very hectic, people all over the place, and then, boom…a baby. He looked like a day-old piece of uncooked chicken. I asked the doctor is he was sure he was done cookin'. Nobody appreciated my humor. Nobody ever appreciates my humor. Admit it, people…you'll miss me when I'm gone! And it is OK to admit that newly born babies just don't look right. Yuck!

To say Tommy was a handful in his infancy would be an understatement. The child had two settings, screaming and sleeping, and he didn't do much of the latter. That boy would scream and scream and scream and scream and…sorry…I think I was having a flashback there. He drove me insane. Nothing we did made him stop crying. Day after day it went on. I can honestly say, and I think Renee will agree with me on this, that had Tommy been child number one, there never would've been a child number two. Dad would often ask me what I was doing to the boy to make him scream, as if I were sitting there poking him with a knitting needle. Nothing, Dad…the kid is just a little ass. In Dad's defense, sort of, he wasn't around when me or my brother were babies, so he never had to experience what a baby who is constantly crying is like.

But there he was. A son. Wow…I finally put the stem in the apple. But what do we do? We've only had girls for the past decade. Do we even know what to do with a boy? Too late. He's here. During the pregnancy, we once again debated names. This time the girl's name was easy…Rose Anne. No need to stray off course now. That was a solid flower name to complete the trio. Or coven of witches…whichever you prefer. Renee would surprise me by not advocating for Jacob, but instead requesting the name Gaetano, pronounced Guy-ta-no. Interesting. You went with my grandfather's name. I like it. But "Powell" isn't an Italian last name, and I felt it would seem a bit off. Besides, since Renee was having her tubes tied during the c-section this time, ensuring this really was the last child we would ever have, this was the last chance to carry on my name. I advocated hard for Tommy Lee Powell III. Renee viewed her attempts to prevent that name from being chosen like someone who was trying to break a chain of evil…jokingly, of course. But she realized this was the last chance to carry on the name, and the lad would officially be given that name. There were now three Tom Powells walking the earth. This could get weird.

Now we were now a family of five, and we had our son. We were saddened to learn that the day care center both girls had attended, Lighthouse Kids, was closing. We so much wanted Tommy to attend daycare there because of the excellent job they had done with our girls. Judy, the owner, and her entire family, were like extended members of our own family, and they were so amazing with the kids. When the girls got to kindergarten, their time at Lighthouse had them fully prepared for the school environment. Eventually we found a good center for Tommy, and he managed to make a lot of friends there that I'm sure he'll still have years down the road, but it just wasn't Lighthouse. Judy, I want you to know that Renee and I appreciate the manner in which you took care of our girls. The program you ran at Lighthouse truly gave them a head start on life, and we always knew they were as safe with you as they would be if they were at our own parents' home. Thank you.

It was when we moved to Channahon that we also began taking annual trips to Holiday World in Santa Claus, Indiana. The girls absolutely loved it the first time we went down, and the lad has grown to be fond of it as well. It proved to be the perfect end of summer get away for our family. We rent a cabin at Lake Rudolph right next door to Holiday World and the kids have a blast making s'mores, watching the golf cart parade, and hitting the putt putt golf course. The cabin sleeps eight, so my sister-in-law, Michelle, and my mother-in-law started making the annual pilgrimage with us. The town is very small, and severely lacking on places to eat out, but we quickly learned that surrounding communities had plenty of dining out options available, and therefore we didn't have to cook all our meals in the cabin. As for Holiday World itself...well the kids all instantly fell in love with the place the first time they visited. Maggie and my mother-in-law always hit the roller coasters because they are both coaster lovers. Renee and Michelle spend most of their time in the lazy river. Lily basically wants a funnel cake and the ability to ride one of their water coasters as many times as possible before heading home. Me? Well I'm a wave pool kind of guy. I hit the water slides and take in some amusement park rides, but a vast majority of my time is spent in the wave pool. Drinks, parking and sunscreen are all free, and the cost to feed a family inside the park is very reasonable, so it rapidly became a very affordable destination for us to end the summer school break. Before you ask, no...I was not paid to mention Holiday World. It has just become such a big part of our family's history, and I love the place so much, that I felt it had to be mentioned in the story of my life. After all, we've been there nine times and have no intention of stopping now. We've even investigated getting a place in Santa Claus, Indiana so we can go more than one time a year. To anyone from Holiday World that may read this book, keep doing what you're doing. It's a winning business model and you have customers for life in this house. You guys have been great over the years.

Channahon would also be the town where my daughters started their non-profit endeavor, Teddy Bear Care. When her grandmother was battling cancer, as you will read about in the next chapter with more detail, Maggie would sometimes go to the hospital with her. It was there she noticed a lot of kids with bald heads battling this deadly disease. It touched her. The winter after their grandmother would pass, the girls asked the pastor at church if they could set up a collection box to collect stuffed animals to take to kids in the hospital. Maggie couldn't bear the idea of being in the hospital and feeling alone, so she wanted to make sure kids had something to make them feel better. Maggie and Lily collected 42 stuffed animals that Christmas season. After the holidays came and went, they asked me if they could keep doing it. I told them that was between them and the pastor. After all, it wasn't my church. But they had something else in mind. They wanted to approach local businesses about having donation boxes in their establishments year-round. Renee and I were rather impressed with this act of selflessness. So, the girls created a presentation and began approaching businesses. They have a few boxes placed around town and, to date, have collected and delivered over two thousand stuffed animals to hospitals including St Joes, Silver Cross, Bolingbrook Hospital, Morris Hospital, as well as others. I couldn't be prouder of their efforts to help others.

I even ran for Park District Commissioner here in Channahon. It was shortly after we first moved here. I didn't know a soul, and nobody knew me. Still, I donned my suit and tie, grabbed a clipboard and went house to house collecting the necessary signatures to get on the ballot. I came in third place with just over five hundred votes. Not bad for a no-name on his first try. While I haven't run for public office since then, I have helped in other ways. I served as the vice-chairman of the Three Rivers Business Alliance for four years and donated my time, and that of my crew, to the special needs day at the local town festival. Recently I was asked to be part of the Comprehensive Plan Advisory Committee, which is a group of citizens from all walks of life that have been tasked with advising the village board on a new comprehensive plan for our town's future. I am honored to be a part of it. Channahon is a great community that really provides one with many options for helping their neighbors. If you are abled bodied, please find a way to donate your time to one of the local causes in your town. And if you're looking for a great place to raise a family, come check out Channahon.

"AS YOU GET OLDER THREE THINGS HAPPEN. THE FIRST IS YOUR MEMORY GOES, AND I CAN'T REMEMBER THE OTHER TWO." – SIR NORMAN WISDOM

CHAPTER ELEVEN
Living with The Fugitive

This chapter is about the last four years of my father's life...which just so happened to be the four years he lived with us. Those who don't know my father, or his story, might read the title of this chapter and wonder if my father was wanted by the law. He wasn't. At least not in his later years. The name of this chapter is in honor of my father racing days. As I detailed earlier in this book, dad was a drag racer. He had many cars, and, as racers do, he named them. There was "Powell's Demon," "Jrs Toy," and he had multiple cars that bore the name "The Fugitive." The Fugitive was Dad's "street name" back when he and my Uncle Jake were illegally racing, so he carried it over into his professional racing.

By the time Tommy was born, Dad was already living with us for a few months. The series of events that would lead to Dad living with us were set in motion back in the summer or 2009. Jo was out with Dad and some friends one night when they noticed she looked a little yellow. Dad arranged for her to see a doctor, and tests were run. That's when Jo was diagnosed with stage two pancreatic cancer. It was a blow to the gut. Dad had always been the one in and out of the hospital, not Jo. This wasn't supposed to happen to Jo. Jo was always the one sitting bedside for another one of Dad's hospital stays while we kept her calm about any potential outcome. But this time it was Jo. It was real, and it needed to be dealt with. It was agreed upon that Jo would undergo the "whipple" surgery. This was a major procedure. We needed to be ready to help Jo through this. My main priority in life became trying to keep my father sane while Renee began researching everything she possibly could about pancreatic cancer. The day of the surgery was nerve wracking. Dad was a caged animal. Constantly on the edge. As they wheeled Jo away, she made me lean over and then asked me to promise not to let anyone put her in a nursing home. Talk about a weight on my shoulders. Wow. But I couldn't say no to anything Jo would've requested. She earned whatever she was asking for. If she didn't want to go to a home, then Goddamnit, she's not going to a home. Jo didn't want to go to a home because she had to put her dad in a home years before, and she hated the fact that she had to make that decision. She hated the fact that her dad wasn't in his own home. Her dad had slowly developed Alzheimer's and she just couldn't meet his daily needs anymore. But she shouldn't have felt guilty for one moment. She made the decision she had to make, and that woman didn't go a single day without visiting her father in that home, unless she was out of town on vacation. She literally went every day. She was as devoted a child as you will ever see. So, I understood where she was coming from by asking not to be put in a home. But let's get through the surgery first.

Several hours later, she would be out of surgery and on to recovery. Recovery would be followed by chemotherapy. Chemo took a little out of Jo, but she fought through it. She managed to get out here and there and was battling as hard as she could. But round one of chemo was soon followed by radiation therapy. Radiation took its toll. Her decline was far sharper during that period of treatment. She was becoming weaker and more frail. And Dad was becoming more and more concerned. Dad never handled any kind of change very well, and these were some major life changes he was living through. Eventually radiation would end, and an examination would be done before round two of chemo was set to commence. It was then that Jo was informed that they hadn't gotten all of the cancer from the surgery. It was still in her. All they could do now was push on with the next round of chemo, and hope for the best. She was admitted to the hospital for a round of chemo, and it was during that time that I received a call from my father telling me he was driving himself to the hospital because he couldn't breathe. Because that's what rational, sane people do...they drive themselves to the hospital when they can't breathe rather can call an ambulance. I once again found myself back at the hospital, only this time Jo was on one floor while Dad was on another. I would spend my day bouncing from floor to floor making sure each of them had company and everything they needed. It was becoming exhausting for me. One day I grabbed a nurse and asked to speak to the highest-ranking person on the floor. I began rattling as many cages as I could until I finally got Dad and Jo put not only on the same floor, but in the same room. It was much easier on me that way, and it allowed the two of them to see each other. It was funny and sad all at the same time. They would eat their meals by pushing their hospital trays together and would argue over what they were going to watch on TV just like at home. It was like their own personal nursing home suit. Eventually Dad would be released, followed by Jo. Her treatments were completed. Now she had to go home and hope beyond all hope she would beat the 4% survival odds.

Her children, Ray and Denise, were advised to make arrangements to get to Chicago as soon as they could if they wanted any time with their mother before she passed. Thankfully, they both made it in time to have those few last conversations with their mother. Catch one more Cubs game on WGN together. Talk about how there's always next year for their beloved Cubbies one more time. Making sure they told each other how much they loved each other one more time. Jo deserved that. She deserved the comfort of her family being around her in her own home at that moment in her life. She had given so much to so many for so many years, she earned every second of that borrowed time. Jo passed away on July 28th, 2011. I'll never forget that night as long as I live. During that stage of Jo's decline, I was making regular trips in to Berwyn to lend a hand in any way I could and be there for Jo and my father. I had been in to visit them earlier in the day and had since headed home for the night. It was shortly after I had returned home that Dad called and told me that Jo just passed. I immediately turned around and went straight back. It was dark, and it was raining, and we needed to deal with his right now. My step-brother and I called the funeral home, but they were closed. We tried every different number we could find. None of them worked. So, we decided to go to the funeral home, and see if anyone was there, or in the apartment above it. Like fools, we pounded on doors and windows all the way around that building, in the rain, trying to find anyone that was available to help us. At one point, my step-brother, Ray, looked at me and said "Well, we'll never forget this night as long as we live…that's for sure." Man, was he right. Eventually we found who we needed to find, Jo was picked up, and I returned home. I left behind a stunned and rattled father of mine. His world had just collapsed. He couldn't stand to stay in the house anymore. He needed to get out and put it behind him, but ultimately, he never was able to put it behind him. I don't think anyone really ever can truly put something like that behind them. He had known Jo since he was in high school. They had a lot of history together. And now she was gone. He literally moved in with us the very next day. Our lives were all about to change forever.

Prior to Jo's diagnosis, everyone, including my father, agreed that Jo would outlive Dad, so we had several family meetings about planning a future without Dad, and what we were going to do with Jo. When Jo got diagnosed, those family meetings shifted to begin discussing what we were going to do with Dad once Jo passed. And yes, Dad and Jo were part of all of those meetings. I had some private conversations with my father as well and he had determined well before Jo passed that he was going to come live with us in Channahon. So, Dad was ready to make the move the moment Jo passed, and he showed up at our place July 29th, 2011…the day after Jo died. Life comes at you fast.

When Dad moved in, we became a family of five, with a baby on the way, in a three-bedroom ranch. Something obviously had to be done. We looked for houses that would accommodate our family, but ultimately decided to remodel our house to make it fit the family. We were in the tail end of the recession so buying a new house wasn't an issue. Waiting to see how long it would take to sell our current home became the obstacle. We couldn't sit on two mortgages for any period of time, so we remodeled. Picture, if you will, our situation in that moment of our lives. The girls' grandmother had just passed away, Dad had moved in with us, Renee would give birth in just four months, and we were embarking on a full house remodel. Chaos is the only way to describe those four months. Utter chaos. If you ever have the choice between that scenario and shaving with a chess grader, go with the cheese grater. Our house was basically the worst parts of the bible playing out on a daily basis.

But, we endured a full remodel, and lived to tell about it. And now we had the room we needed. Finally. Once the construction was completed, and Tommy was born, we set out to figure out a day to day existence that would work for everyone. Not an easy task to accomplish, to say the least. Slowly we began to figure out something that worked for all parties involved, but when it really began to work better for the whole family was when Dad switched all of his doctors from Loyola to St Joes. The commute back to Loyola was just not going to work in the long term. If Dad wanted to continue to drive into Melrose Park for his haircuts, that was his issue. But we needed to be at these doctor's appointments, and the drive was just killing us. Once everything was moved to St Joes, everything started to work...sort of. Dad was still able to come and go as he pleased at this point, and the doctors were close enough for us to get to the appointments, so all we needed to work on a routine inside the house. That took more effort. Dad had a habit of doing dishes or vacuuming his room very early in the morning on the weekends, so we would often argue about that. He constantly felt like I was trying to control him, and I constantly felt like he had no respect for the fact that he was in our house. Looking back, I now realize how hard it must've been for him to no longer be the king of his own castle, and I could've handled things better. The man made daily trips to the same stores over and over again. He would have cases of Starbucks ice coffee and oranges in his closest. You've never seen anything like it. When the oranges would run low, he'd just come out with another case from his closest like he's running a mini-Walmart in there. I understand the need to keep busy, but he continuously resisted our attempts to get him engaged in some sort of activity in town. We wanted him to meet some new people out here and maybe enjoy his time a little. Instead, he made friends in some local places around town just by frequenting the establishments regularly. He quickly made friends with one of the women at Casey's, but Dad seemed to creep her out just a tad. It was almost as if Dad was looking for a girlfriend. He was flirting with her the way he used to with my mom back in the early '70s. Weird. He also became good friends with the staff at a local diner called Lonestar. He would come in for lunch and sit in the booth off to the side where the waitresses would sit. He would shoot the breeze with them as they came and went and would discuss the latest world news with the owners as they sat and watched the TV together. He was there so often all the waitresses knew his order by heart. For a brief period of time, he may have actually enjoyed a little bit of life. Not much, but a little. But wherever he was, and whatever he was doing, Jo weighed heavy on him at all times. Many times, he told me it should've been him that went first.

As the months went on, Dad would have his ups and downs. Whenever we would be approaching a significant day in his life with Jo, he would become unbearable. We understood why, but he was still very nasty towards everyone around him. For a few days before each one of these important days, Dad would begin snapping at everyone. He would snap at the kids when they left clutter around and tell them this place looked like a pig sty. His agitation with dinners, or any lack thereof, would be visible every night. He was a "dinner needs to be in the table at x every night" kind of guy. As you can imagine, our family doesn't always function that way when one kid has a game in Yorkville at the same time the other kid has a game in Kankakee. Sometimes a family dinner doesn't happen. That drove Dad insane. And if nobody was making him food, he didn't eat the way he was supposed to. There were some weeks where maybe we saw him four times all week. And when those periods would fall around special days in his life with Jo, it was almost as if he took it as an insult. We hadn't forgotten the special days, but life continues. We have practices and games to attend. We have school functions and family parties to attend. We still have work that we need to go to in order to keep the roof over everyone's head. And all of that always came before a dinner out for Renee and I. Always. We rarely were we able to sneak away for a simple dinner out during those years.

Dad's agitation for whatever special day it was at the moment would pass and we would slip back into a normal groove again. It was a roller coaster ride from month to month. As his aggravation grew, so did his health problems. He would find himself in and out of the hospital and nursing home rehab centers. He would attend a never-ending string of doctors' visits, and he would always complain that the doctors weren't telling him what was going on with his health. Renee did 99% of Dad's doctors visits after he and I had a massive blow up leaving one of his appointments. That particular incident resulted in me being left on the side of the road in Joliet and having to call Renee to pick me up. I had accompanied Dad to one of his doctor's visits and watched him lie to the doctors about how he was caring for himself. I saw this as a direct affront to me and my family, because we were the ones having to deal with the reality behind his lies, so I spoke out and told the doctor the truth. This enraged Dad, but the doctors needed to know the truth, so they could properly care for him. On our ride home, I attempted to talk to Dad about it, but he refused to speak to me and just turned the radio up. I turned the radio down, and he turned it back up. That resulted in me loosing that famous Italian temper of mine, and I punched the radio and screamed at him to leave the damn radio alone and talk to me. He lost it and pulled over. He demanded I get out of the car. I took the keys out of the ignition and took his house key off the ring and then told him that if I was going to be stuck on the side of the road, he was going to be locked out of the house. When Renee came to pick me up, we both returned home to find Dad waiting in the driveway. All three of us went in and began discussing what happened. Discussing isn't really the accurate description for what happened. It was a full-blown screaming match. It got ugly for a while. It was one of the many times Dad packed a bag and threatened to leave. He believed I was trying to control him like a child. And in a way, I was, because he was like a giant child. He wouldn't do anything the doctors told him to do, he lied to every doctor he had, and he was lying to us. As I mentioned earlier, he visited Casey's a lot, and it turns out he was having hostess cupcakes with iced coffee. He thought we didn't know, until I saw the debris in the garbage can outside. Since I knew the people that worked there, I asked the Casey's employees if my dad was coming in there and they told me he was, in fact, a daily regular. I asked if he was buying the cupcake and coffee and they told me it was what they called the "Tom special" because he got it every day. I became a lit fuse. Here we were running around to endless doctors' appointments, fighting an uphill battle with his health, and he was hurting his own cause by having cupcakes and iced coffee every day, and then lying to us, and the doctors, about it. It led to another screaming match. At this point, my father and I were pretty much at each other throats on a daily basis. I was fighting him to make sure he lived, and he was fighting me because he had obeyed doctors' orders for decades, and in the end, he finds himself alone and miserable. Looking back, I understand that when someone has had enough, it's time to just let them live how they want to live. But at the time it was my job to keep him alive, and I was failing at that job. I had never failed at my jobs before, so I employed every tactic and measure I had at my disposal to be successful at this task, including screaming and yelling. It got real bad for a while. Real bad.

One of the things Dad did that made me furious was that he paid extra attention to Tommy. I have no doubt that he loved all of his grandkids, but Tommy was a little special to him. Maybe it was because he was a boy, or maybe it was because he carried on Dad's name, but whatever the reason was, it was wrong for him to do. He would always ask the girls how their day was, but usually not until they had been home for a couple of hours. Tommy was asked as soon as he walked in the door. As we would eat dinner, Dad would turn his chair away from the table, and thus, the rest of us, to watch Tommy play in the living room. That boy had Dad so wrapped around his finger, that he would go into Dad's room, demand Dad get out of his chair, and then change the channel, and Dad would obey him. This began to wear heavily on the girls. They could see that Dad was doting on the lad, and they didn't like it. And to be honest, I can't blame them. Here they were sharing a room, so Dad had a room for himself, and he's ignoring them in favor of the boy. It just wasn't right. No matter how much we told him he was doing it, he just never could see his actions. To their credit, the girls just sucked it up and kept on moving forward with their lives. They never rocked the boat with him, and they always helped. Maggie has found Dad more than a couple times when he's fallen or passed out.

Renee would do her best to make sure Dad understood everything the doctors were saying, but that was an uphill battle as well. It was partly because Dad just didn't want to listen to any more doctors, and partly because his doctors were from other countries and had deep, deep accents. I'm surprised Renee didn't come out of that period of time being multilingual. So, after each failed attempt to explain to Dad what another doctor had said, she would just smile, nod, and move on to the next day's issues. It was all she could do to keep her own sanity. She had her own pressures being a very important player at work, being a mom to three kids, and becoming a referee for the fights between my father and me. I'm sure she will be nominated for sainthood one day. Saint Renee of the Arguing Powell's. Patron saint of dumbasses. Renee would become Dad's lifeline, and he did his fair share of embarrassing her. When Dad called a nurse with a Polish accent a Nazi, it was Renee there cleaning up the mess. When Dad threatened to pour water on his roommate at the rehab center because he was snoring too loud, Renee was called in to calm everyone down. When Dad would tell a doctor the only reason he was in Dad's hospital room was to pad his bills to pay for his rounds of golf, Renee was there to ease the tensions. He didn't make it easy on that woman. Not one bit.

With Dad in and out of the hospital and rehab, Renee got to know a lot of nurses and hospital staff and, as a result, she knew which people would tolerate his shit and which people wouldn't, and she became good at playing the chess game of managing Dad's anger with these people. Without Renee, Dad probably would've died a year earlier than he did.

As Dad's body continued to break down, he would come to face new challenges he'd never experienced before. One day, he passed out in the bathroom, first falling forward, and then sideways. We couldn't get the door open from the outside because his body was laying up against it inside the bathroom. I had to use all my strength to push the door, and his body, far enough away to allow Maggie to climb through the opening and pull Dad's body away from the door. Once he was found in the hallway, bleeding and passed out. He had passed out the night before watching a march madness game, hit his head, and crawled as far as the hallway before passing out. We found blood on his bed, chair, carpet, and wall that time. He even had an incident at the local diner that caused him to be carried out by paramedics. One Easter morning we were woken up to the sound of Renee's phone ringing. It was the emergency room doctor at St Joes asking about Dad's medication. Renee was baffled. Why the hell is an ER dude talking about Dad's medication? It turns out Dad was having a breathing issue, so he called the ambulance himself without waking us. He got dressed and waited in the living room for them. When they arrived, he met them in the driveway as not to wake us. We were dumbfounded. Absolutely floored. I mean, who does that?

One morning he became too anxious to get to the car while Renee was getting ready to take him to a doctors' appointment, so he decided to try it without help. He opened the screen door and placed his walker out on the front porch, propping the screen door open. He then went to take a step out but lost his control and fell backwards…except his leg didn't cooperate. His foot stayed on the ground, bending his knee back and snapping it. And with nobody behind him to catch him, he fell all the way back and snapped it good. This would be the event that ultimately kicked off his final days alive. The injury he sustained in that fall would require knee surgery. The surgery was scheduled and Dad, as always, was oh so pleasant in the days leading up to it. The surgery went relatively well, but when he had to return to have the wounds cleaned on a follow up visit, it was revealed that Dad had "limited" blood flow to his legs. Limited? That's a joke. He had ZERO blood flow below the knees. So now he had an open surgical wound, as well as a couple of other open wounds on his legs and feet, that wouldn't heal. They weren't getting any blood. We were told that if he kept up with his home health rehabilitation exercises it might help, but it was a long shot. To me, a long shot is better than no shot, so I began really pushing Dad to do his rehab. I would insist he do his exercises and he would yell at me to stop treating him like a child. I knew he was going to die if he didn't work his ass off to regain his strength and I just couldn't get him to see it. At least that's what I thought. He saw it. Now that I think back to that time, I know he saw it. He saw it and was done with it. He had listened to every doctor tell him everything he didn't want to hear for over thirty Goddamn years and he was done listening. They took away his sweets and his Dr Pepper. They took away his salts and limited his bread. They shoved pill after pill after pill down his throat for decades. They had him giving himself insulin and they poked him full of holes at the appointments. They cracked his chest open and performed major surgery on him. They've placed mechanical devices attached to his heart inside him to keep him alive. They cut out so much of his insides that when he was placed back together, they had to do new X-rays and MRIs to map out where his internal organs really were because they no longer resided where they were supposed to be. He spent enough money at hospitals to have one built bearing his name. He was done. And nobody was going to tell him differently. But, once again, I was tasked with keeping alive. I was told to make sure he would be able to watch his grandchildren graduate from high school at the very least. I had a job to do. I made promises. We don't back down on our promises here. We do the jobs we have to do, and Goddamn it, that man was going to do his fuckin' therapy if I had to drag him to the sink and move his arms ala "A Weekend at Bernies." He wasn't having any of it and I wasn't backing down. At some point, factors had to be introduced to change the equation. Those factors came in the form of Dad being given some very limited, very shitty options from which to choose.

Choice number one: In order to prevent the several various infections currently residing in his legs from passing through his entire body, and eventually killing him, he was going to have to lose one leg above the knee, and one leg below the knee. He would become 100% bed ridden for the remainder of his days, completely dependent on others for survival. OK...that's a shitty option, so let's hear option two. Turns out, option one is the only option in which Dad lives. What? Woah. I need a minute. When a team of doctors lay that one on you, it's time for a cigarette and some thinking. I couldn't believe it. You mean I can't just push him harder and get those legs to work again and save him from being a double amputee? Nope. His legs were too far gone. They were infected, not healing one bit, and had to go. Now I sat and watched the realization of what was just explained to us wash over my father. A man that raced cars professionally. A man who worked three jobs and still played on the company softball team. A man that has now been told in order to live, he can never walk again. It was as if someone hit all of with a coal shovel right upside the head. How the hell were we going to care for a bedridden, double amputee? If they take his legs, the only option becomes Dad permanently residing in a nursing home. It was the only way. We simply didn't have the time, nor resources, to have him stay at home in that condition. Holy shit. Life comes at you fast.

Choice number two: voluntarily admit yourself into hospice care, be taken off of your array of life sustaining medications, and slowly die. Everything that was wrong with Dad was managed through medication, and half the medication he took was to counteract the effects of the medication he had to take initially. Better living through chemistry, right? Without any of his medication, parts of him would begin to fail and eventually shut down completely, and he would be gone in days. Option two sucked as much ass as option one. So that's it? Never walk again or die? So, a man busts his ass his whole life, takes care of his family, suffers heartache and turmoil his entire life, and in the end, he's rewarded with never walk again or die? Life really sticks it in and breaks it off. One of the big reasons why I am an atheist is because I refuse to believe a god would let garbage like this happen to people.

As I looked at my father, I could tell he had already made up his mind. He was not struggling with making the decision, he was struggling with figuring out how to tell me. Our early fights, when he was still self-sufficient, were really about control. It was a dick measuring contest between my father and I and we were whippin' them out daily. But towards the end, the arguments, I would come to realize, weren't about power. He was trying to die, and I was fighting him. He understood the mission I was trying to complete, but he just wanted me to let him die. I realized it the moment he turned to me and said he wanted to go to hospice, but he needed me to tell him it was OK to die. He literally said those words to me. He knew this meant I would fail at my mission, but that was ultimately inevitable anyway. That's when it hit me…he just wanted someone to tell him he didn't have to do it anymore. I felt like shit for having pushed him. I pushed him for us. I pushed him because I wanted him to see Maggie graduate. I pushed him because I wanted him to see Lily get her license. I pushed him because Tommy was so attached to him that losing him would be devastating. And I was pushing him because he was my dad. That was what I was supposed to do. He did it to his dad. But that pushing only delayed his suffering. He kept going to doctors and putting himself through all of that because he didn't want his son to fail. I had to look at him and tell him I wouldn't be mad if he decided to die. It was the single hardest thing I have ever had to do in my entire life. It sucked. It still sucks.

So, after assuring my father I wouldn't be mad at his decision, I handled all of the paperwork to get him over to hospice. I stopped pushing him to live and handled everything to allow him to die. He was moved into a hospice room at the Joliet Area Hospice Center just days before his 70th birthday. All of his medications were stopped, and his dietary restrictions were lifted. That man was so happy to be able to eat whatever he wanted again. He was happier than we had seen him in a very long time. His body began to swell from fluid retention, but he made it to his birthday. All five of us would spend a good portion of that day, July 4th, 2015, with Dad in his room. We played cards, ate brownies, and told stories to celebrate the old man's 70th. He wore the honorary red white and blue hat and we were able to get some nice pictures of him with the kids. By the next morning he would have declined so badly, that he was unable to speak or eat. He was just laying in bed struggling to breath. Right or wrong, I made the decision not to bring the kids back after that. I didn't want their last memory of their grandfather to be of him struggling to breath. Four days after his 70th birthday, Dad would pass on July 8th, 2015. We had a small, one day service that Dad arranged when he came to live with us and he was cremated afterwards. His ashes sit in my office at home in a wooden urn that I picked out when I assisted Dad in making his final arrangements. I have now lost both of my parents and all of my grandparents. When you are a kid, your parents are the ones having to deal with elderly parents who are dying. They are next in line. When your parents go, it falls to you to handle everything because you are next in line. Now they are all gone, which means I'm next up. My children are now who I was just a few short years ago. That is a stark reminder of how short life is.

Perhaps one day I'll write a book about the four years Dad lived with us, because there are so many more stories to tell about that time in our lives, but for now, I want to end this chapter with some actual Facebook posts by Renee during that period of time. These posts are quoted exactly and cover a variety of incidents and conversations with Dad.
Enjoy.

August 14th, 2013
"I'm pretty sure that I just secured my sainthood status. Just took an 8-year-old AND an almost 70-year-old to Walmart, neither of which can keep a thought to themselves. Literally, they were saying to each other, wait, one

more thing…. because their conversations to me were that important. Also, for public record, my eulogy should make note of at least a dozen times I was a saint."

February 3rd, 2014
"I bet none of my family or friends knows that my father-in-law had a 234 average. I'm calling bs, otherwise he missed his calling in the PBA."

March 30th, 2014
"Attention all bowlers: my father-in-law asked Maggie how heavy her bowling ball was. When she said 12, he said his was 28. Must have gone along with his 234 average. I need a drink."

May 25th, 2014
"In case anyone was wondering, 1971 was the year that they let women start drag racing. According to my father-in-law, it was horrendous. The fact that I only managed to say, 'I don't give a flying fuck about racing', and then walked away, shows an amazing amount of restraint on my part. That was a table flipper moment."

November 7th, 2014
"Attention everyone in the Chicago area: my father-in-law says we are going to get 5-8" of snow because his I-thingy said so."

January 30th, 2015
"Another reason why someone needs to be there during admitting:
Nurse: Do you have a living will?
Pop: Yes
Me: No, you don't
Pop: Yeah, Jo and I made one
Me: That's a last will and testament
Pop: I was living when I made it
Nurse: Do you have a DNR?
Pop: Ummm
Me: No. Pop, it's a 'do not resuscitate'
Pop: Yeah…try to bring me back. Unless I'm going to be a vegetable, then don't
Me: He does not have, nor does he want, a DNR"

Tom Powell Jr.

"DON'T BE AFRAID TO GO OUT ON A LIMB.
THAT'S WHERE THE FRUIT IS." – JACKSON
BROWNE

CHAPTER TWELVE
The man, the legend, the entrepreneur?

Roughly four months after Dad moved in, and just days before Tommy was born, I lost my job. I had been working for Walsh Landscaping when they abruptly went under in the early winter of 2012. When I took the position with Walsh, it seemed like a dream come true. It was $18,000.00 a year more than my last position, it was closer to home by about an hour, and I would be working on much larger commercial projects. It was perfect. The owner of the company was a bit odd in that he worried about the strangest things. For example, we weren't allowed to leave our laptops on our desks overnight. He thought it made for an untidy looking office. We had to close the laptop, put it in the carrying case, and have it neatly tucked beneath our desks every night. No personal photographs of any kind were allowed on your desks. All of the blinds on all of the windows around the entire office building had to be opened the exact same amount, as to create a pleasant looking building from the exterior. We weren't allowed to back our trucks into the parking spaces, they had to be pulled in nose first, because he didn't like the look of a backed in truck. If we were exiting the truck to come into the office, we had to get rid of any drink cups we had in our cup holders. I was literally pulled out of a production meeting once to be told that a cup was found in the cup holder of my truck, and that it was unacceptable. We're talking really off the wall shit here, folks. The owner had grown up in military schools and was wound tighter than a two-dollar watch. We had to wear khaki pants only, and all shirts had to be pressed and tucked in at all times. And no hats. Had he spent a little more time watching the bottom line instead of our shirt collars, maybe he'd still be in business…but I digress.

This loss of income was particularly troubling for many reasons. First, I had only been with them for ten months after leaving a position I was in for ten years. I left a secure job for this? Second, I had a house payment, three kids at home, my ailing father just moved in, and we just dropped a massive amount of money in rehabbing the house. How was I going to earn? What was I going to do? This was bad. Very bad. I was submitting resumes to every large landscape firm in the Chicagoland area, whether they had an ad out or not, but it was a month before Christmas. Nobody was hiring. Around the Chicago area, landscapers don't start hiring mid-level managers until after the new year. I had to just wait out the holidays and hit the job search hard in January. My anxiety levels began to climb as the holidays came and went, and the prospect of a new landscape season was just a few short months away. That's when Renee looked at me one night and suggested I start my own company. My immediate and stunned response was to remind her that we had a newborn, my elderly father living with us, and we were still climbing out of a recession. She was going to have to excuse my bluntness, but I should've taken her for a drug test right there and then. But despite my fervent push back, she persisted with the idea. She kept trying to sell me on the fact that I had the experience, and we'd saved the money, and now was as good a time as any. My father also offered to help pay some bills here and there while I was getting the company up and running. I was just really hesitant, but I began doing some research on used equipment anyway. In my searching for various equipment options, I came across a young man name Arturo who was selling a complete landscape setup. He had started his company as a freshman in high school, with his father putting the equipment in his name. He mowed lawns throughout his four years in high school and had recently graduated and was set to attend school to become a heavy equipment diesel mechanic. After a little negotiating, I ended up purchasing from Arturo his truck, trailer, two commercial mowers, one string trimmer, a lawn edger, an aerator, a hedge trimmer, a plow, a salt speeder, and sixteen lawn accounts. All in, we made the deal at $14,000.00. I took the plunge and began marketing myself to gain more clients. Now I was really nervous.

Soon I would find myself signing clients from here in Channahon, as far west as Morris, as far east as Lemont, and as far north as Naperville. I managed to piece together a pretty solid base of mowing customers. In that first year, it was all residential customers. Now I just had to get some labor, and we could go to work. I reached out to Jimmy...yes, that Jimmy... and I set out to dominate the world. I picked up one more laborer, OG Kevin. OG's interview would become the classic stuff of legend. I knew OG's mom, and she suggested her son as a possible laborer when she learned I was looking to add a laborer to the crew. OG and I spoke on the phone and we agreed to give him a sort of "on the fly" interview on his first day. Kind of an interview and field audition all in one. As he approached the truck that first morning, it hit me that Jimmy and I were both smokers, and maybe this young college man wouldn't want to be in a work truck all day with two guys that smoke like chimneys. So, I did what anyone would do, I asked him if he smoked. His response was "Smoke what?" Being a lover of the sticky icky myself, I instantly identified that as the response of a fellow herbal lover, and boom...interview was over. He had the job with those two words alone.

After picking up OG, we began to add little jobs here and there, but that first year was really difficult. As it turned out, 2012 was one of the worst times to start a landscape company. That year saw the worst drought in nearly eight years, and I spent half of the summer getting called off because lawns weren't growing, and nobody wanted new plantings until we saw some steady rain. Go figure...I finally have my own landscape company, and we hit a massive drought that was killing the landscaping industry in the upper Midwest. Like I said...it was a rough first year.

Towards the end of the first year, Jimmy bolted, as Jimmy tended to do, and I finished out the season with a filler. This was now the second time Jimmy screwed me. I was pissed. I had dealt with him being late constantly, and always having an excuse. I even worked with him so that he could meet us one day a week at a job site that was within biking distance from his house. But still the excuses came. One day he didn't show up. I called him several times but got no answer. I finally went to his in-law's house, where he was living, and asked if they knew where he was. They said he was with me. Obviously not, or else I wouldn't be standing in your living room looking for him. His mother-in-law went upstairs only to find him passed out in his room.

He came racing down the stairs when he was informed I was there. You could tell he had been partying all night and he was still feeling the effects. His eyes were bloodshot, he was staggering, and he seemed incoherent from moment to moment. He demanded we go outside and talk, which was the exact moment I knew I was about to be fed a line of bullshit. He told me that he was on the bike path to my house early that morning when he was stopped by a cop for being on the path before sunrise. He then told me he was arrested because he had some weed on him. He actually expected me to believe that he was stopped, arrested, taken to processing in Blue Island, for some reason, was able to call a buddy of his, that buddy subsequently drove to Blue Island to bail him out, and then managed to get Jimmy back home…with his bicycle…and Jimmy still had time to fall asleep. Now if we put aside, for a moment, that Jimmy wasn't going to be bonding out of any jail on a marijuana charge considering he was a felon, there is still a massive problem with the timeline. All of this, according to James, took place in under an hour and a half. Come on, man. I may have been born at night, but it wasn't last night. But, I needed the labor, so I brushed it under the rug. Then came the day he called to tell me he couldn't work for me anymore. The person who was giving him a ride to work had gotten a job themselves and could no longer drive Jimmy to work. I offered to pick him up and drop him off every day but told him he needed to pay for the gas. His reply to me was "So now I have to pay you to work for you? Fuck that!" No, Jimmy…you have to pay for the gas that is getting your ass to and from work every day. But he just didn't get it. He never got it. Such a waste of potential he was. He was intelligent, did well in school, and was a good football player, but he pissed it all away for a life of parting, and just never grew up. That was the last dealing I ever had with Jimmy. Decades of on-again, off-again friendship, years of traveling together, and countless hours of partying together was all over. I just couldn't deal with it anymore. I grew up, and he never did. Jimmy called me in March of this year to tell me he was in rehab and to ask me for a job. I'm glad he is finally getting some help, but I am all out of help to give him. I've used up all of my good will when it comes to Jimmy. He is on his own from now on.

Heading into season two, I was pleased to have OG Kevin back in the mix, along with another full timer, The Closer. That crew managed to do some pretty damn good landscaping. The Closer's weapon of choice was a scoop shovel affectionately referred to as The Bitch. OG Kevin took a big step forward in honing his maintenance skills, and the crew was shaping up to a formidable force. We were kicking ass and takin' names. In early summer I received a call from a promotion company that was in charge of hosting an event in our local town every year known as The Warrior Dash. They were looking for a local company to perform the landscape restoration of the land they were about to destroy on one of the local farms. Naturally I jumped at the chance and was pleased to learn that I had landed the job. To say it was a unique experience would be selling it short. I had never seen anything like this before in all my years of landscaping. The course was a massive adult obstacle course, that included a giant slip and slide down a very steep hillside. Restoring that hillside was a unique adventure unto itself. I remembered the first day we arrived, OG and The Closer accidentally let one of the rolls of straw blanket get away from them, and it raced down the hillside at Mach two. Then you could almost see the light bulbs go off above their heads...straw blanket roll race! The next thing I know, several rolls of straw blanket were heading down the hillside, along with OG and The Closer, who were running down the hillside at full speed to see if they could beat the rolls to the bottom of the hill. They lost. But, we eventually settled down and managed to put that hillside back to its original shape. Restoring the mud pit at the finish line was another interesting endeavor. The things we found at that finish line still astonish me. We must have found over three dozen race medals, several pairs of glasses, a mountain of shoes, a few bras, a pair of underwear, and at least one phone. I remember thinking to myself "These people really just left all of this behind?!?!" I still have several Warrior Dash medals in my workshop that we found that day. And the views on that job were spectacular. Looking out over the river atop the hill at Dollinger's Farm made for some peaceful breaks. The Closer was a solid worker and an all-around good guy, but he had some quirks. That man would literally fall asleep in the middle of a conversation while driving in the work truck. He was passed out on the way back from every job. Hell...he'd sleep during the short trips between lawn maintenance accounts. I've never seen anything like it. And for whatever reason, he thought Burger King tacos were good. It would drive me bonkers watching someone eat Burger King tacos as if they were eating actual tacos. But, to each his own.

At the beginning of season three, we had a lot of work on the schedule, so we added another guy, Big Red. Red had helped us out on a mulching job the year before and proved he could carry his weight, so adding him was a worry-free decision for me. With the addition of Red, now we could, and did, take on much bigger projects. I have to say, looking back at some of the projects we did that year makes me proud. We really amped up the quality and saw customer satisfaction spike. We got called to stabilize some slopes on a peninsula lot in Plainfield. The house was a magnificent structure that towered over the lot, affording you views of the water from wherever you stood. The owners had an amazing in-ground pool installed, with a zero depth walk in, attached hot tub, and negative edge waterfall. It was stunning. We would day dream about hitting that pool each hot summer day we worked there. The customers arranged to have their own wild seed mix delivered, and we were there to provide the labor. The prepping of the slopes was relatively easy, which provided us with a false sense of confidence as we headed into the seeding and blanketing portion of the project. After some trial and error, and more than a few wet feet from going in the pond, we developed a system where two men were at the bottom of the slope, and two men at the top. The top two would push a roll of straw blanket over the edge and let the gravity of its fall do the blanketing for us. A few staples at the top and bottom, and it was secure enough to move on to the next section. Once we had the entire slope blanketed with just the stabilizing staples, we then returned over the whole slope, adding staples in key locations to really secure it to the slope. At one point, OG and The Closer were holding Big Red's feet as he hung, head first, down the slope, putting in staples as he spider-crawled along the slope. Look…I never said we were the brightest crew, but we damn sure one of the most innovative.

This was also the year of the Noto project. What a job. The customer already had a landscape plan done, and had the trees and sod installed. What he needed now was the understory plantings. But the plan needed to be tweaked first. We made some wholesale changes to the plant selection and layout, and then went to work. We installed over five hundred shrubs and nearly two hundred perennials and grasses, as well as dozens of yards of mulch. It was a stunningly beautiful project. It was also when I acquired our hand auger. With so many holes to dig, a gas-powered auger only made sense. But even a small one-man auger can take its toll on the arms, so the guys developed a two-man system that worked like gangbusters. Before you knew it, they were cranking out holes at a lightning pace. Day after day, more of the project came together, and you could begin to see the magnificent creation we were leaving behind. The guys worked their asses off, and also took a lot of pride in what they had done. And rightfully so. It was awesome to see these young men take the same kind of pride in creating something so beautiful out of nothing, just as I had done when I first began landscaping many years before. When all was said and done, the customer treated the crew to some pizza and beer at the end of the last day, and we all just sat and gazed at the finished product in all our exhaustion. I never felt prouder of my guys than I did at the end of that project.

As we entered season four, we saw The Closer head off to other opportunities, so we added Big Christian to the crew. This was a man among boys. And to show you I'm not embellishing, he once manhandled, by himself, pieces of outcropping stone from the truck to their place within the landscape, that would normally take two men and a tree dolly to move into position. Now we had some serious muscle to go with the seasoned experience of OG and the energetic nature of Big Red. We knocked out some more really nice residential work, but we also took on a lager HOA property. This was a true test for the guys in the maintenance department. This was nine straight hours of mowing just one property. The site consisted of entrance common areas, several large ponds, and a clubhouse. I loved the site. You could get on your mower, pop in the ear buds and just go to town. The site proved to be a profitable one as well. From an efficiency standpoint, it was a dream. We are up an entire day on the maintenance schedule, and we only had to move the trailer within the confines of one site. We were even able to pick up additional projects from the customer in the form of mulching some areas as well as adding some plantings to other areas. The company was really running smoothly at this point, and I was very pleased with the results. OG was now good enough to run a crew. And Big Red was a machine on the sites. The two of them would just be on auto pilot and watching them work was a site to see. Big Christian was new to the game, but he was keeping up with the old pros more and more as the season progressed. By the end of the season, however, he had had enough and left the company. He thanked me for the chance, and he went on to other opportunities. OG, Big Red, and I finished out the season, and we headed into the winter having just had a very good season.

Now we were heading into year five. After Christian departed, it was now down to the three of us. We were light one guy. Now that I've had time to look back at that situation, it was actually the best move possible. It got the company lean without losing any of our ability to take on larger projects because OG and Big Red were now seasoned vets. Anything I threw at them, they handled with ease. They were also now going out on smaller projects more and more without me. I cannot tell you what a comfort it is, as a business owner, to have a crew that you completely trust to get the job done, and never fails to live up to the task, day in and day out.

As the season wore on, my relationship with the property manager of that large HOA went off the rails. I was called out to discuss why I had not trimmed any of the shrubs at the clubhouse, yet we were clearly looking at freshly trimmed shrubs as we toured the grounds. It didn't make any sense.

So, I took pictures of everything he pointed out as evidence he was asking me about shrubs that were already trimmed. Then the weirdest thing happened, and it proved to be the turning point for the whole relationship. The clubhouse had a sand volleyball court that had been overrun with weeds since we took over the project the year before. I would periodically email the property manager asking if he wanted us to remove the weeds as that wasn't something they wanted covered in their original contact. I was consistently told no, and the property manager would tell me that the HOA was so damn cheap, they would never approve it. And if they didn't care how it looked, why should he? Well I cared. It was my truck in that parking lot and the people passing by who saw the weeds didn't know it wasn't in my contract. As far as they knew, I just wasn't doing my job. It made me look bad. But still he refused. Then, out of the blue, I was asked if I could de-weed the court. Of course I can. I've been asking for this for over a year. I even gave him a dirt low price of fifty dollars to do it to make sure we were approved to make this court finally look good. But we were heading into our vacation period, and it had to wait until we got through those two weeks. Every year my crew and I would take two long weekends in a row in August to get away. One Thursday and Friday for me to get down to Holiday World and another Thursday and Friday for the guys to attend EST Fest in Ohio. The guys would be pissed if I didn't call out EST and Machine Gun Kelly by name, so here you go guys…this one is for all of EST nation. Lace Up, hippies! Each year I would send emails to my customers, starting early in the summer, letting them know that we would still be mowing their lawns during these two weeks, it would just be off schedule by two days. I would send these emails once a month to keep it fresh in everyone's head, so it didn't come as surprise. Every one of my customers was always fine with this arrangement, and this property manager was no exception. He would email me back acknowledging the message. But when this weed removal project came up, he snapped at the notion that it had to wait until vacation period was over. All of a sudden, he wasn't OK with the arrangement he had not only agreed to all summer, but that he had agreed to the previous summer, without objection. Not this time. This time I got a call telling me I wasn't allowed to take vacation time because I was a landscaper. What does that even mean? Are you seriously suggesting my profession prevents me from taking time away to have a vacation with my family? Seriously? Get bent. And we are only talking about four whole days out of the entire summer. It's not like the company was shutting down. We just weren't doing any additional work above and beyond keeping the lawns mowed for those two weeks. But this guy blew his stack. He ended up pulling the weeds himself, with the assistance of some board members while we were away. Whatever. At least the damn weeds were finally pulled. A couple weeks later, he emails me the day after we mowed the site, he copies in his boss and every member of the board and says that we didn't mow three of the ponds. What? We mowed everything. This guy is losing it. The tell-tale sign that he was lying was the fact that he didn't include pictures in his email. This guy took pictures of everything, so I instantly knew something was up. We were wrapping up a lawn in Shorewood when the email came through. I wrapped up what we were doing and made a beeline for the site. He wasn't there when we arrived, so I took pictures of the three ponds and responded to his email with photographic evidence showing the mowed turf around the ponds. I sent these pictures within an hour of him sending his email. Each pond takes an hour to mow. My pictures would surely show him he is mistaken. Wrong. He chirped back that these pictures weren't from today or I had just quickly mowed them and then taken the pictures. Seriously, man…get some help. You're nuts. I then receive another email that evening from the property manager saying that he re-visited the site, saw that one pond was still "not mowed," and one was freshly mowed, which proved we had just been there. He claimed that he didn't have the time to check on the third pond, which he has to pass to travel between the two ponds he claimed to have visited. The bullshit was starting to pile up. Once again…no pictures. The emails back and forth got heated and nasty. The following week the payment was due for the next month's service, and for the first time in a year and a half, the check was late. I'm no mathematician, but even I can do the math on this one. Something had changed. So, I called the office and asked what was up. After catching some bullshit excuses, I told them service was suspended until payment was received. I was done playing games with these people. I didn't work my ass off to finally have my name on the door to have some lying property manager tell me in not allowed to take two days off a year for vacation. Fuck. That. Nonsense. After doing some last-minute scrambling, the owner of the property management company said he would have the property manager hand deliver the check to my home that night. I informed them that if he stepped foot on my property, he was going to be arrested. I was done with these people. I ended my email by offering to forego the thirty-day cancellation notice in the contact and just let them find someone else to service their site for the remaining time left in the landscape season. They accepted the offer and, thankfully, we went our separate ways. To show you how aggravated I was with the garbage from them, the balance on that contract cost me over $13,000.00 in revenue that year. And it was worth every penny that was lost. Sometimes you just have to acknowledge that a particular customer is simply not worth the headaches and cut your losses while you can. The rest of my time working for myself was so pleasant after we rid ourselves of that jobsite. It was as if a giant weight had been lifted off of everyone's shoulders. It was the best move I made in the six years I had the business.

In year six, it was the same three-man crew again, and once again we were running lean, but highly efficient. Once again it was OG, Big Red, and me. The guys, who were now known as Kevo Squared, were now heading out to do more jobs on their own, allowing me to begin strategizing about future moves. My goal was to keep it simple that year and just continue to bang out really nice work. And we did just that. The accounts were looking better than they ever had, and the customer base was happy. I was feeling very free not having that property manager over my head. I was relaxed. Almost too relaxed. As happens every year, we got our big construction job for mid-summer. This time it was the installation of the landscaping for the new putt putt golf course going up in town. I really enjoyed that project. We installed hundreds of shrubs and perennials, over a dozen trees, and over one hundred tons of decorative stone. The job worked the guys like never before. We brought in a hired guy, Joey Bag O Donuts, aka Veggie Tales, to lend us some much-needed additional muscle. Even my eldest child, Magnolia, was out there digging holes. The days were long, very hot, and back breaking...but the end result was very nice. With the layout we chose, along with the material picked, the course will really have some nice, natural flow to it once everything reaches full maturity. The autumn brilliance Serviceberrys will be seen up and down Rt 6 when in bloom and will absolutely burst with fall color. I really can't wait to see this project once it has matured. The maintenance during this season was steady, solid, and everyone paid on time. The weather was cooperative, and we had a lot of very productive days. It was also in year six that we met Bud, the man who owned our new dump site. Bud was local to the area, had a farm outside of town, and exchanged the right to dump there for some new plantings and mulch in the front of his house. Bud is a great guy. Always smiling, seemingly without a care in the world, and always with his dog, Murphy, at his side. Murphy was a very unique dog. He was a pit bull that was as strong as an ox, and as playful as a toddler. He had a variety of toys he would want you to throw around the yard for him. From time to time, he would jump up into the truck with us as we were dumping. The dog had the strangest habit of eating grass clippings. I've never seen anything like it before. Murphy and Bud were inseparable. And then, one day Bud informed me that Murphy had aggressive cancer and needed to be put down. All of us were devastated for Bud. You could really see how hard it was hitting him. Bud's wife has passed away years ago, and while his son was still around, Murphy was his everyday companion. They went everywhere together...and now he was gone. It got to Bud so bad that he sought counseling. But in the end, Bud introduced a new dog into his life. Beasley the Rottweiler is now at his side wherever he goes. And Beasley is just as playful as Murphy ever was.

We got to experience some crazy things during our time together, and not all of it work related. Take, for example, the fact that it was during this time period that we all got to witness the impossible...the Cubs winning the World Series. While the guys and I would bust each other's chops about hockey vs football, we all agreed on loving that moment in Chicago baseball history. I can remember thinking how tired I was going to be the next day while sitting through that rain delay in game seven, but with the outcome being what it was, the next day at work was like walking on a cloud. Everyone had a constant smile on their face. They did it! They won the freaking World Series! In our lifetime! One of the best sports moments of my life as watching Bryant make that throw to Rizzo to seal the deal, and then Rizzo pocketing the ball. And for those Cubs haters who will be reading this, I have but one thing to say to you;
"Go, Cubs, go! Go, Cubs, go! Hey, Chicago, whatta ya say, the Cubs are gonna win today!"

All of the guys that every worked for me will always hold a place of gratitude from me and my family, but the two that were specifically instrumental in the company's success were the duo known as Kevo Squared. Even though they would boggle my mind by telling me they never heard of Jerry Garcia or didn't know who some of the world most influential people were, they never failed to make the work day enjoyable and profitable. Their work ethic and loyalty is something I will never forget. They have both since moved on to other careers, and I wish them both the best of luck in everything they attempt in life. I will offer them just a few words of advice at this time...never try to be who someone else wants you to be, always follow your gut, and never change who you are. You are both dynamic young men with incredible futures ahead of you. This is your time in life...seize it. And from me and my family, I thank you for all of the hard work you put in. And now, to honor Kevo Squared, I shall impart to you some of their words of wisdom.
"Ya can't toss chest high sueys without learnin' the fundies of chuckin' the biscuit." Words to live by, folks. Words to live by.

"WHAT'S SO FASCINATING AND FRUSTRATING AND GREAT ABOUT LIFE IS THAT YOU'RE CONSTANTLY STARTING OVER, ALL THE TIME, AND I LOVE THAT." – BILLY CRYSTAL

CHAPTER THIRTEEN
Remaking a legend

One thing that never really occurred to me, in all my years of working, was the possibility of walking away from landscaping before I was a ripe, old man. After all, it had been my life's work for so many years. It was such an integral part of my life that it is how everyone knew me. I was Tom the landscaper. Hell, landscaping is such a huge part of my life that my daughters are named after flowers. For as long as I could remember, I wanted my own landscape company. I loved idea of finally being able to run a company the way I always thought one should be run. I longed for the days when I could leave my mark on the industry, and not just work to line other people's pockets. At this stage in my life, I had everything I ever wanted. A great family, a nice house in a great community, and my name on the door. But as the years have progressed, my exuberance for the job had diminished little by little. There was a time that when we hit mid-February, I was chomping at the bit to get back to work. I could feel the creative juices flowing and I could almost smell the first load of mulch coming off the truck on a chilly spring morning. Those were the moments I once lived for. Don't get me wrong, I hadn't lost my love of landscaping, I was just getting more and more drained. Renee noticed it. She could tell that the wear and tear of two decades of hectic landscape schedules had worn me down. I was preparing for another season, but I just wasn't thrilled by it this time.

As I was enjoying my winter break between the summer landscape season of 2017 and the spring thaw of 2018, Renee and I began to contemplate what the coming years would bring. What was our plan? Where did we want to see ourselves in twenty years? What options are available to us? This caused us to revisit some of our prior goals and compare them with the current times we were in. Renee had spent the better part of a decade climbing the ladder in her industry to the point where she was now in charge of a facility, something very few women do in the historically male dominated sector she was in. This, as one would expect, resulted in her compensation reaching levels we never could have imagined. It supplied an economic comfort that allowed us to look at my landscaping and ask if we even needed my income anymore. We didn't. So, with me approaching forty-six years of age, and having put in over two decades in the field of landscaping, Renee suggested that maybe I wanted to seek out other avenues of self-employment that aren't as taxing on the body and could possibly refresh the mind. Business opportunities that we wanted to pursue earlier in life, but never did.

Initially I thought the concept was insane. I mean, I'm a landscaper. That's what I do. If I wasn't going to be landscaping, what the hell would I do with myself? I'm not really skilled at anything else. Spring time rolls around and I head back out to earn…that's the way it goes. Needless to say, the idea of walking away from my life's career was both nerve wracking and almost inconceivable. So, I processed all of the various possibilities laid out before me and began weighing the pros and cons. Throughout the process, I continued to talk to prospective customers, and interview potential employees. I still had to be prepared to start the season. Each night drew some more conversation about what would be best for our family between myself and Renee. I was racking my brain trying to figure out the best move. It didn't feel right to have Renee shoulder 100% of the income burden while we waited for a new company to begin generating revenue, but she was making so much money that my income became irrelevant. And she wasn't about to quit working. The thought of being home all the time just didn't appeal to her. And now the ownership group that controls her company is expanding yet again, which opens up even more earning potential for her. She had truly climbed to the top in her industry. She can now write her own offer letter anywhere she goes. That's a damn good feeling to have when you've busted your ass to be where you are. She started out as a merchandisers assistant for a rival company when we first moved to

Channahon. The pay was ok and at the time, that's all we really needed. Her work ethic and drive soon would be on display and she was moved up to a logistics manager position. Along with the new title came more money, and more hours. We would constantly butt heads over her hours and the people she worked for. I felt like they were taking advantage of her, but she was just concerned with keeping a paycheck coming in. It wouldn't be too long before they would fire the facilities manager and lean on Renee to keep things afloat. She did, and soon they brought in another facility manager. This sequence of events would continue and manager after manager would be brought in, and subsequently fired. And every time they would lean on Renee to keep things moving. After one manager was let go, Renee asked why she couldn't get the manager's position and run the facility. They, in a roundabout way, informed her that this was a man's' industry, and a woman wasn't going to be running any facility. I thought she had a legal case, but she just started floating her resume around. She was called one day by a headhunter who saw her resume on a job board. She conducted an initial "meet and greet" phone interview with her, and then set up a face to face meeting with the owner of the company. He had heard of her through industry connections, and was very interested in bringing her in. He was planning on building a new facility from the ground up, and was looking for someone to oversee its construction, and eventually run it. At the interview she was very standoffish and felt nervous about leaving a steady job for a facility that wasn't even built yet, even if her last employers were clearly sexist assholes that were never offing to give her a chance based on her gender. Sensing her hesitation, the man gave her an offer she simply couldn't say no to. She oversees that facility to this day and has been a successful, and profitable, manager in a field dominated by men. As a result, her income has reached a level that allowed me to walk away from landscaping without having to replace the revenue. Maybe next time her former employer won't let a set of mammary glands determine an employee's qualifications. Their loss…our gain.

So, I made the decision. I retired from landscaping. We decided that we would take what we had and begin investing it in other business avenues. Make our money start working for us rather than us working for our money. We are exploring several investment opportunities that will also keep some of my time occupied managing those new assets. In the meantime, my primary task is operating the house, handling the kids array of stuff, and dealing with keeping everyone moving and where they are supposed to be.

One major undertaking I have embarked on is once again getting healthy. Anyone that knows me knows that I have been big at different stages in my life. It is something I have battled on and off my entire life. I could always handle being heavy. That was never an issue for me. I always worked, I didn't mind buying bigger clothes, and I carried it respectfully. But recently the bad health has had effects on me I am less than pleased about. One morning, while getting ready for work, I apparently began talking to the guys about the days schedule, then drifted into another conversation, and then hit the deck. OG ran to get Renee, and the next thing I know I'm looking up at everyone asking them what happened. That little episode resulted in Renee demanding I go to the hospital, especially after I almost passed out again in the kitchen a few minutes later. So now it was me, not dad, being taken from the house in an ambulance. Same name…different generation. Luckily for me, we had gotten to know Channahon's Fire and Paramedic personnel quite well over the four years dad lived with us, so it was like seeing old friends. Despite my most charming efforts in the ride to the hospital, the paramedics refused to let me drive the ambulance. Oh well…you can't win 'em all. The end result of all of the poking and prodding was a diagnosis of diabetes. I wouldn't need insulin, but I did need two blood sugar pills and a daily checking of my levels. Now I was poking my finger, just like dad. After watching what he went through, I knew I didn't want to end up like him. I worked a little harder, but still remained big. Then Renee and I decided to go to Jamaica for our twentieth wedding anniversary in 2019, and I decided I was not going to be the fat guy at the resort. I was fixing this right now. I downloaded the My Fitness Pal app and began tracing calories. I combined that with an hour a day on the treadmill and some light dumbbell workouts to get me back up to speed. Soon I found the weight coming off in a nice, steady manner. And I didn't have to try anything goofy. I wasn't on some diet fad plan, nor was I taking some pill. I wasn't rubbing a cream on me or wrapping anything around me. I was still eating frosted flakes for breakfast, and still having a brownie when my late night sweet tooth comes calling. I still eat bread, tacos, and pizza. I just watch how much of it I eat, and it is now balanced with exercise. The heaviest I ever was in my entire life was 344 pounds just a year ago. When I decided to begin this fitness journey on January 18th, 2018, I weighed in at 328 pounds. As I sit here and type this today, I am down 42 pounds, and heading in the right direction every day. I WILL reach my goal weight of 225 pounds, and I WILL maintain it from that moment forward. As a result of my efforts, I am no longer in need of either of my two blood sugar pills. Next stop…eliminating the two blood pressure pills.

As you can see, I also have personal projects that I'm working on, such as this book. In addition, I have other books in the pipeline, including one on the town we call home, Channahon. I'm currently running a weekly podcast that talks about life from the perspective of a husband, father, taco lover and Dead Head. It can be found on anchor.fm. Just search for "The Tom Powell Jr Show". I am also running a blog that can be found at my website, www.TomPowellJr.com. All of this is being run through one of our new companies, The Powell Entertainment Company.

I have also stepped up my help to the girls with their non-profit. My life has been changing over the last few months in radical ways. And Renee and I have some traveling planned, starting next spring with that trip to Jamaica for our twentieth anniversary. Our hopes are to be able to take one long weekend a year to visit a destination here in the U.S. and take one longer international vacation each year. Renee has a lot of domestic cities she hasn't seen yet, and there are untold number of taco stands just waiting for me to enjoy their delicious products before I depart this earth. Get the chorizo ready, folks…I'm coming in hot! We will still get our annual Holiday World trip in as well, as long as we can keep convincing the kids to go as they become young adults. And thanks to my niece, Amber, we now know of a killer little Mexican place near the water park that has some chorizo tacos that are off the chain. Tommy likey. I will be taking up kayaking this summer and plan to continue to release more books that I have in the pipeline. This is all such a radical departure for me that I'm really just getting my feet under me. I can see myself sitting on some local volunteer boards or committees, but not running for elected office anytime soon. It's time Renee and I enjoy the fruits of our labors. We did the right thing and sacrificed to make sure our kids never went without. Now it's our time. While I've traveled all across his country, Renee has seen very little of it. It's time she tastes that Memphis BBQ and feel the history of New Orleans. She deserves to feel the ocean breeze in her face in Seattle and see the wildness of San Francisco. And it's time I saw the word outside of the United States. My traveling days are not over by a long shot, and I have a pretty long list of things I'd like to see before I make my exit from this life. And I have kids to watch get married. I have daughter/father first dances to participate in. I have to teach my son how to shave and not be an ass around girls. So, I'm not going away, I'm just not landscaping anymore.

Throughout your life, different people will come and go who introduce new experiences that stay with you forever. Since music has been such a big part of my life, a lot of my life changing new experiences center around someone in my life introducing me to some new form of music. I'd like to take a moment to tell you about some of the biggest musical influences in my life. As a child, music was always playing in my house, from Elvis to Styx to Boston, so in a way, you could say that my mother was the first musical influence I had. As I grew and aged, I developed my own taste for music that was mainly centered around the pop music of the time. Then I met Jill Krejci in Jr High. She introduced me to hair metal by lending me her copy of Bon Jovi's "Slippery When Wet". She is responsible for putting my feet on the modern rock path. Shortly after Jill, a man named Allen Pokay introduced me to punk rock and opened my eyes to a world I had never known. He is responsible for introducing me to bands such as Naked Raygun, The Butthole Surfers, Screeching Weasel, and Killdozer. I will never forget the hours spent listening to the album "Understand" in his basement. The next major musical influence of my life was my cousin, Jr. He opened my eyes to the likes of Jimi Hendrix, Judas Priest, Stevie Ray Vaughan, Metallica, and Ozzy. Obviously, this would become a major factor in my musical style moving forward. The biggest musical influence on me, bar none, was Jimmy. Yes…that Jimmy. After all, he brought me into the world of The Grateful Dead, and that would forever change my life. He also introduced me to artists such as Poi Dog Pondering, The Freddy Jones Band, and the immortal Bob Marley. Jimmy's musical influence on me cannot possibly be put into words. It is massive. My wife, Renee, also was an influence on my musical life by bringing in country music. It's still not my favorite genre, but it has made its way into my playlists over the years. Many years later, a young man would become yet another musical influence on me, and that would be Kevin Pryor. Kevin brought me to Machine Gun Kelly and EST nation. While I haven't embraced the EST lifestyle as much as Kevin may have liked, I can see that those who reside within the EST family truly do share a common bond centered around music. Perhaps the reason I haven't embraced the movement as much as this generation has is because I already had my EST family in the form of the Dead Heads. Nevertheless, I have a few Machine Gun Kelly songs on my phone and he has proven to be a go-to artist during my daily workouts. Kevin also introduced me to Mod Sun and his Mod Squad. If you see me in your city, say "What's up, my hippie?". I am eternally grateful for each and every person who has introduced me to a new musical sound during my lifetime, and I can't wait to see what kind of new music I will be introduced to by the next person on my life.

I don't know what the future holds for me. None of us do. I expect that in the years to come, as was the case in the years that have gone by, life will continue to come at me fast. But I know this…I've been through enough of what life can throw at you to take on whatever is around the corner.
To quote the Chicago band, The Bad Examples:
"I've been machine-gunned, hand-gunned, hijacked, left for dead…
Dive bombed, napalmed, nuclear war headed…

Dropped from a jet plane, with no parachute…
Shot by a firing squad and raped by a business suit…
I'm dancing on a landmine, one leg left…
I can still crawl and I'm not dead yet."

Bring it on, world.

To be continued…

Peace.
Love.
Tacos.

Here are some of my all-time favorite quotes:

"The world is my church, all mankind my brethren, and to do good is my religion." - Thomas Paine

"A hungry mob is an angry mob." - Bob Marley

"In all things of nature, there is something of the marvelous." - Aristotle

"Fat, drunk and stupid is no way to go through life, son." - Dean Wormer

"OVER!" - Michael Corleone

"I don't eat fast food often, but I love tacos. I could write prophetically about how perfect the taco is." - Ken Baumann

"Religion should be like fornication…best done in the privacy of ones' own home." - Anon

"We need leaders not in love with money, but in love with justice. Not in love with publicity, but in love with humanity." — Martin Luther King, Jr.

"When you reach the end of your rope, tie a knot in it and hang on." - Franklin D. Roosevelt

"Leave the gun. Take the cannoli." - Clemenza

"The journey of a thousand miles begins with one step." - Lao Tzu

"Ya just can't fix stupid." - Ron White

"If opportunity doesn't knock, build a door." - Milton Berle

"The bus came by, and I got on. That's when it all began." - The Grateful Dead

"When a man is freed of religion, he has a better chance to live a normal and wholesome life." - Sigmund Freud

"The difference between genius and stupidity is that genius has its limits." - Albert Einstein

"If your plan is for one year, plant rice. If your plan is for ten years, plant trees. If your plan is for one hundred years, educate children." - Confucius

"I did not attend his funeral, but I sent a nice letter saying I approved of it." - Mark Twain

"Everyone should be able to do one card trick, tell two jokes, and recite three poems, in case they are ever trapped in an elevator." - Lemony Snicket

"I don't think the really heavy stuff is gonna come down for quite a while" - Carl Spackler

"Do not go where the path may lead, go instead where there is no path and leave a trail." - Ralph Waldo Emerson

"If you don't know where you're going, any road will take you there." - George Harrison

"Let us remember: One book, one pen, one child, and one teacher can change the world." – Malala Yousafzai

"When fascism comes to America it will be wrapped in the flag and carrying a cross." – Sinclair Lewis

"What a long, strange trip it's been." - Jerry Garcia

Thank you very much for buying this book and reading my life's story. I cannot tell you how much the support is appreciated. Although I never imagined myself writing a book, I had a lot of fun doing this project. I am already looking forward to my next book release, which I have already begun working on.
Stay tuned!

To see more of my content, you can find me on:

The web: www.TomPowellJr.com

Anchor.FM podcasts: The Tom Powell Jr Show

Twitter: @TomPowellJr

Instagram: tompowelljr

YouTube: Tom Powell Jr

Facebook: Tom Powell Jr

Tom Powell Jr.

This has been a production by;

The Powell Entertainment Company

P.O Box 747

Channahon, IL. 60410

This last page only exists because my friend, Dawn Prignano, insisted on having a standalone dedication page, so here it is.

This page is dedicated to my favorite Prignano...Patrick.
You can thank your wife for the idea of a dedication page, ya stunad. Now go run a lap!

GO COLTS!

Tom Powell Jr.